CIMA

INTEGRATED CASE STUDY

PRACTICE

WORKBOOK

OPERATIONAL LEVEL

FOR EXAMS IN 2015

First edition 2015

ISBN 9781 4727 3567 6
e-ISBN 9781 4727 3517 1

British Library Cataloguing-in-Publication Data
A catalogue record for this book
is available from the British Library

Published by

BPP Learning Media Ltd
BPP House, Aldine Place, 142/144 Uxbridge Road
London W12 8AA

www.bpp.com/learningmedia

Printed in the United Kingdom by RICOH UK Limited

Unit 2
Wells Place
Merstham
RH1 3LG

Your learning materials, published by BPP Learning
Media Ltd, are printed on paper obtained from
traceable, sustainable sources.

Contents

Topic 1 - Welcome to the Integrated Case Study

1 Welcome to the Integrated Case Study

What role does the ICS exam play in the 2015 Syllabus?

It complements the Objective Test exams – having demonstrated their detailed technical competence in the OT exams, the ICS exam enables CIMA to ensure students can put their theoretical understanding to use in a real world situation.

The ICS exam enables CIMA to assess important competencies like the ability to communicate appropriately and consider impacts of decisions across a whole business.

It contributes to CIMA's aim of producing competent and confident management accountants – in passing the ICS exams, students show that they can perform well in real world situations.

What's the ICS exam format, and how does it differ from the Objective Test exams?

They are very different, and this means you need to prepare in a different way:

Objective Test Exam	Integrated Case Study Exam
Per paper	Per Level
Computer-based	Computer-based
On Demand	Quarterly sittings
Auto-marked	Human-marked
Immediate results	4-5 week turnaround
All component learning outcomes	High-level themes from each paper
Short OTQs	Long-form "Tasks"
Technical/theoretical focus	Competency/application in the real world focus
70% pass mark	60% pass mark

How will the ICS exam span the three pillars?

The three pillars of the CIMA Syllabus are there for a reason. They are the different dimensions a business must consider to be successful. The relationship between these will be reflected in your ICS exam.

ENTERPRISE	PERFORMANCE	FINANCIAL
• How do we develop strategy? • How do we plan for its effective implementation? • **ARTICULATE A VISION**	• How do we ensure that our strategy is realistic? • How do we monitor activity to ensure that strategy is being implemented effectively? • **GROUND IT IN REALITY**	• How do we prepare financial statements? • How do we interpret financial statements to understand our performance and to help us make decisions? • **REPORT ATTAINMENT**

What role will the student play?

In the exam you will be asked to take on a role, and this varies in seniority depending on the level of the qualification. Here's CIMA's official guidance:

CIMA Level	Perspective	Domain knowledge and integration	Other skill
Strategic	A CFO communicating to a range of internal and external stakeholders	Based on analysis of strategic options (E3) including their risks to the organisation (P3). The analysis is extended to include how to adequately fund the strategy (F3).	External communication, non-financial information, future-oriented. Research skills to focus on both overload and lack of data. Show how to turn data to insight through analysis and judgement.
Management	An accountant communicating to the CFO	Based on product/pricing decisions and/or evaluation of divisional performance (P2) that take account of our key stakeholders (E2). The decisions will be implemented through projects (E2) and their impacts will feed into the financial accounts (F2). These will be analysed and interpreted to evaluate the performance of the organisation and its parts (P2)	Internal communication, both financial and non-financial information and oriented to the present and the future. Research skills to span both overload and lack of data but will focus more on the former.
Operational	An accountant communicating to his/peers	Based costing and budgeting (P1) that should lead the preparation of financial accounts (F1). Results will be communicated to non-accounting colleagues taking into consideration what they do (E1)	Internal communication. Mainly financial information. Oriented to past, present and future. Research skills to focus on how to identify relevant information and turn them into valuable insight.

What will happen in the ICS exam?

- You will be given access to the preseen case study information six weeks before your exam

- The exam will simulate 3 hours in a working day for the company in the preseen

- You will be presented with Tasks to complete, usually in the form of an email from your line manager

- You will be provided with other "unseen" information as the exam progresses, and you will need to quickly assimilate this with what you already know from the preseen.

- You will need to type in your responses to the Tasks set, usually in the form of an email response to your line manager

- Tasks are timed (usually 30min – 1hr each), and you will be automatically moved on to the next Task when the timer counts down to zero

- You cannot go back to a previous Task when the timer has reached zero

- You can 'skip' to the next Task whenever you wish, but you do not bank any time – ie your total exam time will now be less than three hours

What therefore are the key elements of an ICS exam?

Exam Technique	Time management will be very important in the ICS exam, as will your ability to quickly identify what is being asked for in a Task and structuring your answer accordingly
ICS exam environment	Becoming familiar with working in the ICS exam environment will be a great benefit in preparing for the exam
Core competencies	The Tasks in the exam and the syllabus areas they focus on will give you the opportunity to demonstrate your competence in Core Accounting Skills, Business Acumen, People Skills and Leadership Skills
Integration	You will be expected to move smoothly between the pillars, and provide coherent answers that consider all perspectives
Real preseen	You need to understand the real case study sufficiently such that you can place yourself in this world in the real exam, and therefore ensure everything you type relates entirely to the case study organisation. You will effectively be working for a different company for three hours in your exam!
Technical Knowledge	It is very important to remember that you have already demonstrated your detailed technical competence in passing the exams (or being exempt) for the individual papers in the level. The ICS exam will not test you again on the finest detail of the technical theory, instead it will check you can demonstrate how a management accountant adds value to a business in very practical terms in the real world.

How can I study effectively for my ICS exam?

Do

✓ Produce a study plan. The study window for the ICS exam is pretty condensed so you need to ensure you have a study plan that works for you.

✓ Try to think in an ICS way when you're back at work e.g. "what are the impacts of the business deciding to do X?", "how well was Y communicated?", "if I structure my emails like this, will my line manager be able to understand me more clearly?"

✓ Absorb any business news you can – anything from new product launches, to acquisitions and change management issues, big share price changes and legal cases – try to imagine the management accountants involvement in any of these back in the business where it is all happening. Where should they be adding value?

✓ Practice as many Tasks as you can. There are lots in this Workbook! Make sure you learn something from every Task you attempt – having a consistent approach to 'self review' is a good way of doing this, and we'll return to that later.

Do NOT

× Allow yourself to get dragged back into all of the technical detail of the individual syllabus content for each paper in the Level. It's the key themes and topics that you need to have with you for your ICS preparations, and "the factors that need to be considered" in a practical sense when a business is considering applying the theory in the real world.

× Become too wrapped up nor spend significant amounts of time trying to memorise every last bit of information provided in the real preseen case study. Whilst you need to be 'comfortably familiar' with the key elements of the real preseen in time for your exam, you must not go too far with this to the point where it detracts from the amount of Task practice you are doing.

× Try to do everything all at once, or try to remember everything at once from across the whole level. There's too much! You should just focus on one practice Task at a time during your preparations, gradually building up to full mock exams as the real exam draws near.

Topic 2 - Getting up to speed

2 Getting up to speed

Overview

To get to this stage in your studies you have already demonstrated to CIMA that you have the required level of competence in terms of the detailed technical content in the syllabus for each of the three papers in the level.

To allow you to focus on developing the specific skills and competencies you need to be successful in the ICS exam, it makes sense to ensure you are 'up to speed' as soon as possible.

This means ensuring you are still familiar with the key topic areas and themes from your studies of each individual paper, and this Topic will help you to structure how you do this.

Note that it will also help you to quickly become familiar with the four core competencies that are relevant in the ICS exam, and the most effective exam technique you can use to maximise your marks. You can do this by looking at the information included in Topic 3.

Once you are 'up to speed' you can then turn your attention to the all important ICS Task Practice, and subsequently to bringing the real preseen case study into your preparations.

Technical Content from the individual papers

There are two aspects to this. The first is a general one – basically, can you remember the key learning points and main themes from your earlier studies of each paper? The second is a more specific one – what do you need to look at to ensure you have covered the new topics that have come in to the syllabus as part of the CIMA 2015 syllabus update?

1. Refreshing high-level understanding from Objective Test papers

In preparing for your ICS exam through attempting Practice Tasks (see Topics 4, 5 and 6) it will be helpful to ensure you can remember the <u>key themes</u> from the syllabus content for each individual paper in the Level.

With the exception of brand new syllabus topics (see 2. below) you should keep your 'OT refresh' at a high-level, and avoid going back into the detail required for an OT exam.

2.   2015 Syllabus changes – what this means for your ICS exam

Given that the 2015 Syllabus update has seen some brand new topics enter the Operational Level syllabus, and some topics move between papers so they are now viewed from a different perspective, you need something more than a 'refresher' to ensure you are up to speed for your ICS studies.

The information below will clarify for you what is new, or significantly changed, within the 2015 Operational Level, and guide you as to where you will be able to find learning content to help you fill any knowledge gaps in a targeted and efficient way.

Where significant knowledge gaps caused by the transition do need to be filled, that is, on topics you haven't studied in the 2010 Syllabus, you may find that a more detailed approach is necessary to properly develop your understanding of the key themes you need for your ICS studies.

The information below will help you with this.

E1

A new topic called 'Introduction to organisations', worth 25% of the syllabus has been created by enlarging the old section on 'The global business environment'. To make way for this, other existing syllabus sections have been slimmed down by 5%, seeing the removal of political, economic, social context of business / international macroeconomic developments and analysis of major international economies. Alongside this a new section on 'Managing the finance function' has been added, worth 15% of the syllabus. Overall the paper has grown in size and complexity. A further note is the new requirement to complete simple calculations such as growth rates and sensitivities.

IN	Reference to 2015 BPP Course Notes
Organisational structural theory	Chapter 1 (all Sections)
Managing the finance function	Chapter 3 (all Sections)
New IS / IT terminology including 'cloud', 'wireless' , 'systems architecture' and 'Big Data' and the role of emerging technologies and media in marketing	Chapter 4 (Sections 4, 5 and 6) Chapter 10 (Section 6)
New marketing terminology including 'postmodern marketing' and 'B2G marketing'	Chapter 10 (Section 3)

OUT
Political, economic, social context of business/ international macroeconomic developments and major international economies

P1

The focus of P1 has now shifted more towards short-term decision making, with an emphasis on the importance of cost and cost drivers in production, and the use of relevant costs to make short-term decisions. This is also reflected in additional content on forecasting and budgeting, whilst more financial/longer-term concepts such as managing short-term finance and project appraisal have moved to F1 (so remains within Operational Level) and P2 respectively:

IN	Reference to 2015 BPP Course Notes
Explain the principles of decision making including the identification and use of relevant cash flows and qualitative factors.	Chapter 6 (All Sections)
Apply break-even analysis in multiple product contexts.	Chapter 7 (Section 2)
Apply relevant cost analysis to various types of short-term decisions.	Chapter 8 (All Sections)
Analyse product mix decisions, including circumstances where linear programming methods are needed to identify 'optimal' solutions.	Chapter 9 (All Sections)
Discuss the concept of the budget as a control system and the use of responsibility accounting; Analyse the consequences of 'what if' scenarios.	Chapter 11b (All Sections)

OUT
Project Appraisal (to P2)
Managing short term finance (to F1 so still in Op Level ICS)

F1

There has been a repositioning of the F1 syllabus to provide stronger and clearer links to F2 and F3. More specifically managing short-term finance has come in from P1 (but has not changed), and a number of accounting standards have been added, updated or moved in or out of F2. Alongside this the topic of Corporate Governance has been significantly strengthened..

IN	Reference to 2015 BPP Course Notes
Corporate governance principles and approaches in different markets	Chapter 1 (Section 8)
Investment property	Chapter 7 (Section 1)
Government grants	Chapter 7 (Section 2)
Foreign exchange transactions (individual companies only)	Chapter 11 (Section 1)
Employee benefits	Chapter 12 (Sections 1 – 5)
New aspects which impact the preparation of consolidated financial statements: **Non-controlling interest** (including the full and partial goodwill methods)	Chapter 14 (Section 8) Chapter 16 (Sections 1 and 2)
New aspects which impact the preparation of consolidated financial statements: **Mid-year acquisitions**	Chapter 15 (Section 1) Chapter 16 (Section 5)

OUT
The following have moved to F2: IAS 11: Construction contracts IAS 12: Income taxes (deferred tax element) IAS 17: Leases IAS 18: Revenue recognition IAS 24: Related parties IAS 37: Provisions, contingent liabilities and contingent assets Groups: fair value adjustments at the date of acquisition
The following have moved to F3: Share capital transactions

Topic 3 – Preparing to pass

3 Preparing to pass

Core Competencies

Overview

The old-fashioned stereotype of an accountant is someone who is excellent at number-crunching but hopeless at interacting with others. If the accountancy profession really was like this, its members would be unable to compete with the processing power of a computer and become extinct.

CIMA's new syllabus emphasises that, while understanding accounting concepts is crucial to being an accountant, this skill must be exercised in conjunction with other skills if it is to be of real value in the modern business environment. Following comprehensive global research with organisations of various sizes in different sectors, CIMA have developed a framework which shows the skills, abilities and competencies that finance professionals need to help drive the success of their organisations.

The competency framework is based on what today's organisations **expect finance professionals to do**: -

- Perform accounting and finance activities within the context of the business
- Influence the decisions, actions and behaviours of their colleagues
- Provide leadership at all levels

To do this successfully, finance professionals need core accounting and finance skills, business acumen, people skills and leadership skills.

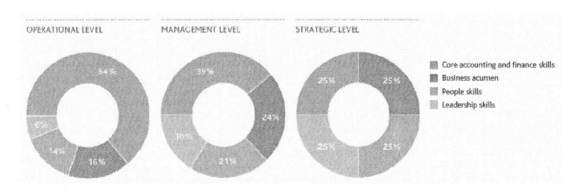

These competencies are underpinned by **ethics**, **integrity** and **professionalism**.

What does this mean for the exam?

In practical terms it means you need to treat the **3 hours of the exam as if you were an employee of the case study organisation**. You need to respond to the exam Tasks as if they were requests from your **real** line manager in **your** real job. The exam is designed to replicate the workplace, as opposed to asking students to provide answers to abstract academic questions.

The good news here is that you have been developing these skills through your life in general and your workplace in particular. The more that you can bring this real life experience into your ICS exam, the more marks you are likely to score. In fact, **the ICS format should naturally incline you to demonstrate these skills**.

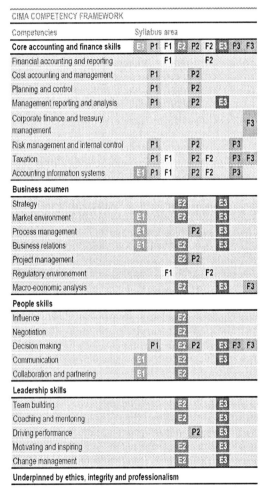

It means that the marks you score for answering questions will be spread across the four competencies, and in passing the exam you are therefore demonstrating you have the skill set that today's organisations require and that you can use what you have learned to make a difference in the workplace.

CIMA have provided the mapping table (opposite) that indicates how the competencies identified in their consultation with employers fit into the overall framework.

In the ICS exam this indicates that the marks you are awarded for Tasks primarily set in the P- or F-pillars will be allocated to the core accounting and finance skills competency in the main, with some in business acumen.

Marks you are awarded for predominantly E-pillar Tasks will be allocated to the business acumen, people skills and leadership skills activities.

In summary, to score good marks in the ICS exam you need to:

- Select the correct techniques and principles to use for the task in hand and demonstrate that you understand them properly (**core accounting and finance skills**)

- You need to so in the context of the scenario as if you worked for the organisation in the question (**business acumen**)

- You need to tailor your response to a Task to the recipient to show that you can communicate effectively (**people skills**)

- You need to make recommendations on how a particular course of action can be best implemented (**leadership**)

Core Accounting and Finance Skills

The thing that makes accountants unique is their ability to use a range of financial and accounting tools. These cover financial accounting and reporting, cost accounting and management, planning and control, management reporting and analysis, corporate finance and treasure management, risk management and internal control, taxation and accounting information systems.

To demonstrate competence in this area, it is not enough to understand these concepts and be able to use them. You will also need to be able to use your discretion to determine which tool is the most appropriate in a given situation and discuss its relative advantages / disadvantages.

Remember – when you give advice to a manager or client, they're not interested in how much you know or how many theories you can mention – all they want is an answer to their problem!

Business Acumen

Commercially valuable advice needs to be tailored to the organisation and environment. While CIMA does not expect any specialist knowledge of real-life political or environmental conditions, you will be expected to demonstrate that you can tailor your advice to a unique environment.

This advice is likely to relate to strategic decision-making, analysis of market and macro-economic environments, process management, business relations, project management and awareness of the regulatory environment.

This competency requires you to review the technical advice you are about to give and consider whether it is realistic given the organisation's condition. For example, there is no point in recommending an expansion strategy to an organisation with no capital operating in a declining market!

People Skills

As an accountant, you will be one of many stakeholders in an organisation who contribute to its overall direction. The other stakeholders are unlikely to understand the complexities of the accountancy solutions you are proposing and, as a result, may not understand the financial implications of their own ideas.

If your advice is to be followed, it is not enough that it is the right course of action. You will need to influence stakeholders, negotiate, make decisions, work collaboratively and communicate effectively if your proposal is to be adopted.

This competency requires you to communicate in an appropriate and professional manner. You may need to demystify the technical content depending on your audience. You will certainly have to communicate clearly and engagingly.

Leadership Skills

The advice that accountants give has implications across the whole organisation and beyond. It is therefore crucial for the accountant to demonstrate leadership if a proposed course of action is to be converted into a meaningful result.

Leadership can take many forms, but will include team-building, coaching and mentoring, driving performance, managing change, and an ability to motivate and inspire.

This competency requires you to understand the likely implications of a course of action on stakeholders other than the recipient and advise on how they should be managed. These stakeholders may not be as clearly defined or rational as the manager or client you are advising, so you will need to pro-actively identify situations where strong leadership is required and then advise on an appropriate course of action.

A note on integration

There are a small number of integration marks that can be awarded in the exam. Its best to think of these as 'bonus marks' that will come from producing **logical** and **cohesive** answers to Tasks in the exam where you have to consider issues and linkages across more than one pillar in the level. If a Task contains two subtasks, each focussing on a different pillar, then the two parts to your answer should complement rather than contradict each other.

Example

Imagine three students each limiting themselves to a single pillar. They would be excellent at their pillar and have a very in-depth understanding of the content. However, they would be unaware of the other two pillars, so their advice, while technically excellent in as far as it goes, would be incomplete.

So, the **P pillar** student would recommend a project with a positive NPV, while failing to recognise that there are change management and financing issues that could derail the project.

The **E pillar** student would recommend a project which motivates staff, while failing to recognise that the overall financial cost will exceed the financial benefit and therefore damage shareholder wealth.

The **F pillar** student would recommend a project with a positive NPV that looks like it could be financed, without adequately considering risk factors or strategic issues.

CIMA want you to demonstrate that you can deal with real life situations that go across all three pillars – ie that you are successfully integrating your learning across the pillars as you move through the qualification.

Exam Technique

Overview

Excellent exam technique ensures you maximise your marks in the real exam. It means you score the most marks you can given your level of understanding of the 'content' by the time you reach the real exam.

The style and format of the Integrated Case Study exam means that **your exam technique will be more important than ever**.

What is it about the ICS exam that makes exam technique so important?

- The ICS exam assumes you have already demonstrated your competence in terms of technical knowledge, so the focus shifts to showing you can deal with "finance professional" tasks in a real world situation

- All the Tasks are timed in the exam so you simply do not have the option of taking longer to produce your answer than the exam timings allow

- You are not allowed to return to your previous answers to make any changes once the timer has moved on to the next Task

- Although you can move on to the next Task before the timer has counted down to zero, you are not allowed to 'bank' any time you didn't use, you will simply now have an exam that lasts less than three hours in total.

- All of your answers have to relate to the case study and be directly applicable to the case study organisation. You have to approach the exam as if you are employed by them, and live in their world.

- You need to ensure you are interpreting the task correctly and doing what is expected by your line manager or whoever is giving you the Task to do.

- You then need to tailor your answers according to the recipient of your email/report

- In order to do all of this really well, planning your answer will be as critical as ever!

So, what does 'excellent ICS exam technique' look like?

It can be captured nicely in our TIPS approach:

Time management at Task level
Identifying the requirement
Planning your answer in context
Speaking to your audience

We'll now look at these in more detail.

Time Management at Task Level

The ICS exam is three hours long, and made up of a number of individually timed Tasks. Your challenge is to be able to produce a good quality response to the task set **within the timings for each individual task**. Given the Tasks will increase in complexity and scope as you move through the qualification, it is likely the 'average' ICS exam will look like this:

	Duration of each Task	Total number of Tasks
Strategic Level	45 – 60 mins	3 - 4
Management Level	45 mins	4
Operational Level	30 – 45 mins	4 - 5

In this time you need to:

1. Efficiently digest the information provided in the Task
2. Identify exactly what is required of you
3. Plan your answer
4. Produce your answer

In order to score good marks for each Task you need to ensure you get to the point where you have at least produced a good and complete response in the time allowed.

BUT – you need to do so without taking any shortcuts in preceding stages, or else you risk your whole answer diverging from the point and failing to respond to the specific requirements of the Task.

It is therefore vital to practice these elements in turn, gradually bringing them together in full Task practice, so that you speed up and find you can hit exam timings come the big day.

Multiple requirements or "subtasks"

When you have identified what is required, you may well find you are being asked to do more than one thing in the allotted time. In this situation you will need to appropriately split your Task time between the different 'subtasks'.

Identifying the Requirement

Unlike the 2010 Syllabus, and the traditional way in which exam questions are presented where the exact requirement is very clearly provided AFTER the question/scenario, in 2015 ICS tasks this will be different:

- Exactly what you need to do may well be spread throughout an email from your manager (eg different 'subtasks' flagged up in different paragraphs of the email) as opposed to the traditional approach of them all being in one place with a helpful box around them.

- Depending on how specifically the task is worded, you may need to exercise some professional judgement as to how to respond, just as you would in the real world. Exactly what is required of you is likely to be pretty clear at Operational Level – but less so as you reach Strategic Level, as the issues faced become more complex.

It is very important that you clearly identify what is required before moving on to the 'Planning' stage. With sufficient practice you will find you can do this with increased confidence and speed.

Planning your answer in context

Having identified what is required, and understood the additional information you have been provided with as part of the Task, you now need to plan how you are going to respond.

NOTE – in the ICS exam you can do this on a Pearson Vue wipeboard – approx 10 sides of laminated white paper, provided to you in the exam with a wipe-able pen. The alternative is to do it "onscreen" – ie as if you were typing the outline for an email before running through and adding all the detail in afterwards. You will need to decide on your preference before the real exam(!)

As part of your planning you will need to consider: -

- What you are being asked to do

- What the key points are that you want to make in your response, and how much detail the request suggests you need to go into

- That you must specifically focus on the **situation facing the company in the question**, such that when you produce your answer in full it relates as much as it can to the scenario.

- How much time you have to do the Task

There are various ways of physically creating a plan, and the best one for you will be a personal preference based on how you like to visualise things. Some people prefer spider diagrams or mind-maps (you'll need to do this with a pen!), others prefer bullet point lists (which you could do onscreen and then transform into your full answer)

The **critical aspect** here is to avoid spending too long producing a very detailed plan that gives you too much to do in the time. Just like in the real world, you will need to limit your communications to the most relevant/important/salient points. Equally, you need to include enough coverage to provide the 'value' that the organisation in the question needs in order to take positive action. This will come with practice and feedback as you prepare for your real exam.

Speaking to your Audience

You will be expected to demonstrate that you can tailor the way you communicate when responding to Tasks, based on the recipient of your response. There are some overlaps here with the People Skills competency, in that CIMA (and employers) want their finance professionals to be able to communicate effectively with the full range of stakeholders in a business.

Marks can and will be awarded in the exam for evidence of 'appropriate communication'

When you are producing your full answer, the main aspect to consider here is whether the recipient has a financial background. If not, then you should look to provide a more fundamental explanation of any of the relevant techniques or concepts in such a way that will help them to understand your main points better.

At Strategic Level, you may be expected to consider the varying perspectives and agendas of different stakeholders and to take this into account in how you construct your response.

As you work through practice Tasks, ensure you think about "how can I phrase my response to make sure the recipient best understands my key points?"

Self Review – How to Guide

Guidance

How do you know you're doing well at work? You wouldn't send a random email to your manager, forget about it and then wait for them to tell you what they thought of it. You'd review your own work very carefully before sending it. You will get the very most out of your Task Practice if you apply the same principles of self-review, especially if you do so in a consistent and structured way.

The role and importance of effective Self-Review

- Will enable you to continually learn as you go

- You need to be effective and efficient in how you study and the way to do this is through adopting the best study habits of which structured self-review is right at the top

- Your answer will never match the suggested solution provided for a variety of reasons, so a line by line comparison is unlikely to yield any useful insight.

- The most important thing here is that you think back on **how you got to the answer**, and whether any problems crept in at an **early stage** – eg on reflection you misinterpreted the requirement or didn't plan properly. The reason this is so important is that improving your approach here will lead to more **marks in the exam for any and every Task!**

- Reviewing your answer **and how you approached it** in a systematic way will help you to focus on specific aspects that you can consciously look to improve next time. This is much more effective than just thinking "must try harder" or "my answer needs to be more like the suggested solution"

The <u>Self-Review Template</u> provided on the following pages is a good framework for doing this

- Print or photocopy yourself further blank versions of this and use it whenever you practice a Task

- Do your initial review BEFORE you look at the suggested solution. Take a step back and ask yourself "how happy am I with what I've produced here?"

- Don't feel obliged to note something in every box for every Task. We'd recommend that capturing 2-3 improvement points is enough for any single Task

- Keep them with you (perhaps inserted in this Workbook) so you can refer back whenever you need to

- In due course you're likely to have more than one attempt at some Practice Tasks – looking at your completed Template from the first time will be a great way of reminding you what you need to focus on during your second attempt (and then you could update your Template with your second review)

Integrated Case Study Tasks – Self Review	Practice Task Ref:
	What did I do well and what will I do even better next time?
Time Management	
Identifying the Requirement	
Planning my answer	
Ensuring set within the scenario/preseen	
Speaking to the audience	
Key syllabus areas	
Other review comments	

Integrated Case Study Tasks – Self Review	Practice Task Ref:
	What did I do well and what will I do even better next time?
Time Management	
Identifying the Requirement	
Planning my answer	
Ensuring set within the scenario/preseen	
Speaking to the audience	
Key syllabus areas	
Other review comments	

Integrated Case Study Tasks – Self Review	Practice Task Ref:
	What did I do well and what will I do even better next time?
Time Management	
Identifying the Requirement	
Planning my answer	
Ensuring set within the scenario/preseen	
Speaking to the audience	
Key syllabus areas	
Other review comments	

Integrated Case Study Tasks – Self Review	Practice Task Ref:
	What did I do well and what will I do even better next time?
Time Management	
Identifying the Requirement	
Planning my answer	
Ensuring set within the scenario/preseen	
Speaking to the audience	
Key syllabus areas	
Other review comments	

Integrated Case Study Tasks – Self Review	Practice Task Ref:
	What did I do well and what will I do even better next time?
Time Management	
Identifying the Requirement	
Planning my answer	
Ensuring set within the scenario/preseen	
Speaking to the audience	
Key syllabus areas	
Other review comments	

BPP
LEARNING MEDIA

Integrated Case Study Tasks – Self Review	Practice Task Ref:
	What did I do well and what will I do even better next time?
Time Management	
Identifying the Requirement	
Planning my answer	
Ensuring set within the scenario/preseen	
Speaking to the audience	
Key syllabus areas	
Other review comments	

Topic 4 – P1 Task Practice

Topic 4 – P1 Primary Tasks

Task 1 - FX

(indicative timing : 36 mins)

You are Tom Smart, employed as a junior management accountant at FX Co. FX is an engineering company which currently produces one type of product, a component for computers, called the CHIP. It is hoped that the company might be able to develop its product range to increase sales. To assist with this the company recently appointed a new Managing Director, John Howard. He was chosen as he has excellent engineering technical knowledge, but he has very little previous financial experience. However he is keen to learn and get to grips with the financial systems used by the company.

The company has an excellent reputation in the market place for supplying good quality CHIPs, but recently a small number of CHIPs have been returned as they were defective.

Today is 1st June 20X5.

You have just received the following extract from the budgeting procedures manual.

FX operates a standard marginal costing system.

Monthly variance reports are produced by the finance function and distributed to the senior management team no later than 5 working days after the month end.

Standard unit cost and price of the CHIP

	$	$
Selling price		250
Direct material (5 kg at $20)	100	
Direct labour (4 hours at $10)	40	
Variable overheads (based on labour hours 4 hours at $5)	20	160
Contribution		90

At the request of the Finance Director you undertake the task of preparing the variance report for May 20X5 and send it the senior management team on 5th June, without any explanations.

The variance report can be found in Exhibit 1.

Exhibit 1

FX May 20X5 Variance report

Output and Sales for May. Budget 1,000 units. Actual 1,200 units

	$	$	$
Budgeted contribution			90,000
Budgeted fixed costs			70,000
Budgeted profit			20,000
Volume variance			18,000F
Expected profit on actual sales			38,000
Sales price variance			12,000A
Production variances	*Favourable*	*Adverse*	
Materials price		6,300	
Materials usage		6,000	
Labour rate	5,040		
Labour efficiency		2,400	
Variable overhead expenditure	–	–	
Variable overhead efficiency		1,200	
Fixed overhead		4,000	
	5,040	19,900	14,860
Actual profit			11,140

Notes:

1   1,200 units were produced and sold.
2   The actual direct materials purchased and used was 6,300 kg costing $132,300
3   The actual direct labour hours worked were 5,040 hours.
4   Fixed overheads have been budgeted at $70,000 per month.

Upon receipt of your schedule, John sends you the following email.

From:	John Howard JH@FX.co.uk
To:	Tom Smart TS@FX.co.uk
Sent:	7th June 20X5, 10.04 a.m.
Subject:	May Variance Statement

Tom,

Thank you for the variance schedule for May, however, I am very concerned to see that actual profit for May is almost 50% lower than budgeted.

Please explain the statement to me and tell me why higher sales have resulted in less profit. Budgeted sales and production are 1,000 units per month, so I would have thought that sales of 1,200 units would have led to higher profits.

Kind regards,

John

John Howard

Managing Director

FX

E: JH@FX.co.uk

T: 0117 900100

Write your response to the email from John.

Task 2 - RDF

(indicative timing : 27 mins)

RDF Co was set up 5 years ago in the UK by Rachel Fisher. Following on from a successful television acting career she formed the company to offer four services to television production companies. Rachel confesses that she is more interested in the artistic performance aspect of the business than the financial performance, but recognises that it is important to make money to keep shareholders happy.

You are Sophie Best, recently employed as a junior management accountant by RDF following the departure of Rachel's old school friend who has been the accountant since the company was founded.

The number of services provided is measured in service units and details of RDF Co's draft budget for its year ending 30 June 20X5 are as follows:

	Service K	Service L	Service M	Service N
Number of service units	1,000	2,300	1,450	1,970
Selling price per unit (£)	18	16	12	20
Variable cost per unit (£)	8	10	13	13
Fixed cost per unit (£)	2	3	2	4
C/s ratio	55.5%	37.5%	-8%	35%

The budgeted level of activity shown in the table above has been based on fully meeting the forecasted market demand for each type of service.

The following chart was prepared by the previous accountant based on the draft budget above.

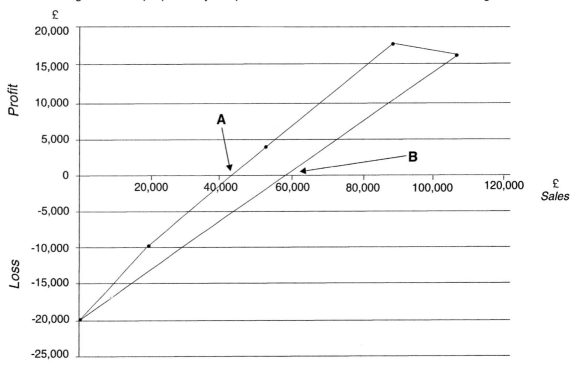

Rachel sends you the following email.

From: Rachel Fisher RF@RDF.co.uk

To: Sophie Best SB@RDF.co.uk

Sent: 7th June 20X5, 10.04 a.m.

Subject: Chart

Sophie,

I have just come across a chart (attached) which was prepared for me by the previous accountant. I have no idea what the point of this graph is or what it has to do with making profits.

Please explain to me the purpose of it, how it can be used to make decisions, and what the points A and B mean, as there does not appear to be a key. It would also be useful if you could highlight the limitations of using it.

Kind regards,

Rachel

Rachel Fisher

Managing Director

RDF

Write your response to the email from Rachel.

Task 3 - BR Co

(indicative timing - 27 mins)

You are Helen Black, employed as a junior management accountant at BR Co. BR is a family owned business, based in the UK, operating from a small factory and rented warehouse. The company was founded by Tony Watts, who originally trained as builder.

The company manufactures specialist insulating products that are used in both residential and commercial buildings. It's best selling product, Product W, is made using two different raw materials – AP and BT.

The company is about to prepare budgets for the next four quarters. Tony is keen to ensure that the company sets robust budgets which can be used to measure performance, as the management team are concerned that BR Co is facing increasing competition in the market place for Product W. As a consequence there have been issues concerning the availability and costs of the specialised materials needed to manufacture Product W, and there is concern that this might cause problems in the current budget setting process.

Sales and customer history

Tony started selling the products to builders' merchants within a 50 km radius of the factory eight years ago. The products have attracted countrywide interest following their use in a building product filmed for a TV company and the products are now sold throughout the UK.

The sales team have forecast expected sales demand for the next 18 months for Product W.

Sales

Selling price	$220 per unit

Sales demand

Quarter 1	2,250 units
Quarter 2	2,050 units
Quarter 3	1,650 units
Quarter 4	2,050 units
Quarter 5	1,250 units
Quarter 6	2,050 units

Purchases and supplier information

Each unit of W uses the following materials:

Materials

AP	5 kgs per unit @ $4 per kg
BT	3 kgs per unit @ $7 per kg

It is BR's policy to hold closing inventory of finished goods equal to 30% of the following quarter's sales demand and closing inventory of raw materials should be 45% of the following quarter's materials usage.

<u>Budgeting system</u>

BR currently uses incremental budgeting.

Today is 4th June 20X5. You have just received the following extract from the board meeting minutes from 15th May 20X5

BR

Meeting Minutes

15th May 20X5

Next meeting: 15th June 20X5

Budgeting

Mr Watts reported that material AP might be in short supply in the coming year. The budgets for the coming year have already been prepared. It was assumed that material prices would rise 4% from the previous year due to inflation. These are shown in Exhibit 1.

As the company has grown and is now coming under increasing pressure from competitors Mr Watts discussed the need to consider the most effective budgeting systems to use and the best methodology for preparing forecasts.

Mr Watts reported BR currently bases it budgets on the prior year figures, making adjustments for any known changes. Mr Watts reported that he has heard that zero based budgeting (ZBB) is an alternative method to use when preparing budgets. Together with the accountant he will explore this further.

Exhibit 1

Production budget in units					
	Q1	Q2	Q3	Q4	Total
Budgeted sales	2,250	2,050	1,650	2,050	8,000
Closing inventories (30% of next quarter's sales)	615	495	615	375	375
Opening inventory	(675)	(615)	(495)	(615)	(675)
(Decrease)/increase in inventory	(60)	(120)	120	(240)	(300)
Production	2,190	1,930	1,770	1,810	7,700

Subsequent to the Board meeting held on 15th May 20X5, Mr Watts sends you the following e-mail:

From: Tony Watts AW@BR.co.uk

To: Helen Black HB@BR.co.uk

Sent: 17th May 20X5, 10.04 a.m.

Subject: Budgets

Helen,

Thank you for preparing the production budget for the next year. I have to admit that I know very little about budgeting, but given that the company is expanding and there is the possibility of material shortages in the coming year I think that I need to focus my attention on it.

It would be very useful for me and also Mr Austen, the Production Manager if you could prepare us a report which covers the following:

- The impact that a shortage of material AP could have on budget preparation and other areas of BR

- If or how ZBB could help us set more robust budgets than the current budget process

- The general problems of preparing forecasts as the basis for the budgetary plan

Many thanks,

Tony

Tony Watts

Managing Director

BR

E: AW@BR.co.uk

T: 0117 900100

Write your response to the email from Tony

Task 4 - Law Co

(indicative timing : 32 mins)

You are Lee Ridley, employed as a junior management accountant at Law Co. Law Co is a solicitors firm which was set up by Phil Webster eight years ago. He performs the role of the managing partner and is responsible for client and staff management, the firm's accounts and compliance matters. He works alongside three other partners who each take responsibility for case matters depending on the branch of law that is involved in each case.

For a number of years Phil has prepared the budgets for the firm. These include budgets for fee income and costs analysed by each partner, and a cash budget for the firm as a whole. The firm has overdraft facilities which are renewable in July each year and sets cash balance targets for each month that reflect the seasonality of some of its work.

At the end of each month there is a partners' meeting at which the managing partner presents a statement that compares the actual results of the month and the year to date with the corresponding budget. At this meeting all partners are asked to explain the reasons for the variances that have arisen.

Today is 8th June 20X5.

You have just received the following extract from the May partners' meeting

Phil informed the partners that he had recently attended a course on 'Budget Planning & Cost Control' at which the presenter argued that each of the partners in the firm should be involved in the budget setting process. He informed the partners that he was going to investigate this further with the management accountant.

After the meeting you receive the following e-mail from Phil:

From: Phil Webster PW@Lawco.co.uk
To: Lee Ridley LR@Lawco.co.uk
Sent: 8th June 20X5, 10.24 a.m.
Subject: Budgeting process

Lee,

As you know I recently attended the course on "budget planning and cost control" which was recommended by our accountants. The course advocated involving the other partners in the budget setting process, but I have to confess that I am not sure that this is a good idea.

The reason I am not convinced by this argument is because I believe that this could lead to budget manipulation. Before I report back to the board I would like you to outline the main potentially beneficial consequences and any potentially adverse consequences of involving the firm's other partners in the budget setting process of the firm.

Another item raised was about feedback and feed-forward control. Please can you explain what is meant by feedback and feed-forward control systems and give an example of each that we could implement within the firm.

Kind regards,

Phil

Phil Webster

Managing Partner

Law Co

Write your response to the email from Phil Webster

Task 5 - GH

(indicative timing : 22 mins)

You are Kate Jones, a junior management accountant employed by GH, a manufacturer of speedboats for sale to the retail market. It has established a reputation for producing quality products which are often recommended It has established a reputation for producing quality products which are often recommended by lifestyle magazines because of their outstanding safety reputation. Currently GH manufactures three types of speedboats.

GH is a family owned business, based in the UK, operating from a large factory, which it purchased 5 years ago. Mr West is the founder of GH. He set the company up 8 years ago after retiring from speedboat racing. Since the boats were designed and launched to the market, he has spent his time trying to increase market share in this niche, but competitive market.

Accounting systems used by GH:

Due to the fact that GH only manufactures three products the accounting systems used are fairly basic. Business transactions are recorded on standard accounting software packages within the factory office by the accountant.

Currently the business prepares an annual budget using standard cost cards. These are produced at the start of each financial year to give an approximation of costs and enable a selling price to be set for each boat.

Budgeting information for next year is given below:

Model of speedboat	Superior £'000	Deluxe £'000	Ultra £'000	Total £'000
Sales	54,000	86,400	102,000	242,400
Direct material	17,600	27,400	40,200	85,200
Direct labour	10,700	13,400	16,600	40,700
Production overhead				69,600
Gross profit				46,900

	Superior	Deluxe	Ultra
Production / sales (number of boats)	1,000	1,200	800
Machine hours per boat	100	200	300

The production overhead cost is absorbed using a machine hour rate.

Today is 20th May 20X5.

You have just received the following extract from the board meeting minutes from 15th May 20X5:

Meeting Minutes

15th May 20X5

Next meeting: 15th June 20X5

Costing information:

Mr West has reported that GH currently uses absorption costing to calculate an estimated standard cost for a boat, whereby total fixed overheads are estimated at the start of the year and an absorption rate per direct labour hour is calculated. Mr West reported that he had heard that activity based costing (ABC) is an alternative method to use in calculating the standard cost for a boat. Together with the accountant he will explore this further.

Subsequent to the Board meeting held on 15 May, Mr West has informed you about wanting to explore the possibility of using ABC. You have already undertaken some work on this and have completed a schedule showing the gross profit for each product under the two different costing approaches. This has been based on your best estimate of the data needed as you have not had a great deal of time. You sent this schedule to Mr West without any form of explanation.

Gross profit using absorption costing

Model of speedboat	Superior £'000	Deluxe £'000	Ultra £'000
Sales	54,000	86,400	102,000
Direct material	17,600	27,400	40,200
Direct labour	10,700	13,400	16,600
Production overhead	12,000	28,800	28,800
Gross profit	13,700	16,800	16,400
Gross profit margin	25.4%	19.4%	16.1%

Superior	1,000 boats	× 100 hrs per boat	= 100,000 hrs
Deluxe	1,200 boats	× 200 hrs per boat	= 240,000 hrs
Ultra	800 boats	× 300 hrs per boat	= 240,000 hrs
			= 580,000 hrs

Overhead absorption rate = Budgeted overheads / budgeted machine hours

= £69,600,000 / 580,000 hrs

= £120 per machine hour

Gross profit using activity-based costing

Model of speedboat	Superior £'000	Deluxe £'000	Ultra £'000
Sales	54,000	86,400	102,000
Direct material	17,600	27,400	40,200
Direct labour	10,700	13,400	16,600
Machining	2,400	5,760	5,760
Set-ups	5,316	7,973	10,631
Quality inspections	1,414	4,242	8,484
Stores receiving	1,800	2,160	2,880
Stores issuing	2,695	3,369	4,716
Gross profit	12,075	22,096	12,729
Gross profit margin	22.4%	25.6%	12.5%

Notes:

The main activities and their associated cost drivers and overhead cost have been identified as follows:

Activity	Cost Driver	Production overhead cost £'000
Machining	Machine hours	13,920
Set up	Number of set ups	23,920
Quality inspection	Number of quality inspections	14,140
Stores receiving	Number of component deliveries	6,840
Stores issue	Number of issues from stores	10,780
		69,600

The analysis also revealed the following information:

	Superior	Deluxe	Ultra
Budgeted production (number of boats)	1,000	1,200	800
Boats per production run	5	4	2
Quality inspections per production run	10	20	30
Number of component deliveries	500	600	800
Number of issues from stores	4,000	5,000	7,000

The machines are set up for each production run of each model.

Upon receipt of your schedule, Mr West sends you the following email:

From: Harry West HW@GH.co.uk

To: Kate Jones KJ@GH.co.uk

Sent: 24th May 20X5, 10.08 a.m.

Subject: Costing

Kate,

Thank you for the budget gross profit schedules you sent me. I have to admit that I know very little about ABC and the basis of your calculations, although I am surprised to see how much difference there is between the profit for the Deluxe and the Ultra when ABC is used.

It would be very useful for me if you could send me an e-mail that explains:

How an activity based costing system differs from a traditional costing system

The possible benefits to the company of introducing an activity based costing system.

Kind regards,

Harry

Harry West

Managing Director

GH

E: HW@GH.co.uk

T: 0117 900100

Write your response to the email from Mr West.

Task 6 - PB

(indicative timing : 25 mins)

Paul Berry opened his own bakery, PB, seven years ago so that he could earn a living from his hobby – baking bread, and has recently employed you, Annie Holmes as a junior management accountant.

Bread making is a traditional process, and Paul still likes to do most of the production using traditional measures, rather than using automated mixers, as he is a naturally cautious person. This has resulted in limited growth despite the local success of his award winning breads; however three years ago PB opened another branch (the South bakery) 10 miles south of the original one and shares his time between them. The original branch is known as the North bakery.

Their signature bread is traditional artisan bread and it has attracted the interest of local food experts.

Today is 28th May 20X5.

You have just received the following extract from the board meeting minutes from 16th May 20X5:

PB

Meeting Minutes

16th May 20X5

Next meeting: 16th June 20X5

Demand:

Mr Berry has reported that demand is up in the North bakery since an article was published in the local press about the traditional techniques used to create the great tasting artisan bread of PB. They are regularly selling out of the artisan bread there, so have increased production.

However, in the South bakery there are unsold loaves of the artisan bread at the end of the day. Demand is uncertain and ranges from 10 batches per day to 12 batches per day. He reported that each batch of bread that is baked and sold generates £50 contribution towards the branches profits, but each batch of bread that is not sold yields a loss of £20. Mr Berry is concerned about waste and the declining profits of the second branch and undertakes to investigate using probabilities to forecast demand more accurately with the accountant.

Subsequent to the Board meeting held on 16 May, Mr Berry has informed you about wanting to explore using probabilities to forecast demand more accurately and calculate the optimum number of loaves to produce. You have already undertaken some work on this and have completed a payoff table showing contribution for the three production levels and applied the probabilities of the three demand levels occurring to the table. You send the tables to Mr Berry without any explanations as you are short of time. (The payoff table and EV table are shown in Exhibit 1).

Exhibit 1: Payoff Table (South bakery)

		Batches baked		
		10	11	12
	10	500	480	460
Batches sold	11	500	550	530
	12	500	550	600
Best outcome		500	550	600

EV Table (South bakery)

			Batches baked		
		P*	10	11	12
	10	0.3	500	480	460
Batches sold	11	0.5	500	550	530
	12	0.2	500	550	600
EV			500	529	523

*the probabilities are based upon sales records for the South bakery

Upon receipt of the tables you have prepared Mr Berry sends you the following e-mail:

From: Paul Berry BP@PB.co.uk

To: Annie Holmes AH@PB.co.uk

Sent: 24th May 20X5, 10.18 a.m.

Subject: Production levels

Annie,

Thank you for the payoff table and EV table you sent me. I have to admit that I know very little about the basis of your calculations, although I am surprised to see that making 12 batches every day is the best option (as it gives us the highest profit of £600 per day) – because producing 12 batches per day was contributing to the losses for the South bakery.

It would be very useful for me if you could send me an e-mail which explains:

What the figures in the tables mean and what "EV" means .

A recommendation of the number of loaves to bake each day in the South bakery.

Many thanks,

Paul

Paul Berry

Managing Director

PB

E: PB@PB.co.uk

T: 0117 900100

Write your response to the email from Paul Berry

Topic 4 – P1 Primary Tasks Solutions

Task 1

	Marks	Marks
Marking scheme		
Explanation of variance schedule		
Sales volume contribution variance	2	
Sales price variance	2	
Materials price variance	2	
Materials efficiency variance	2	
Labour rate variance	2	
Labour efficiency variance	2	
Variable overhead variance	2	
Fixed overhead variance	2	
Maximum for explaining variances		__16__
Explanation of profit variance		
For explaining how the budget has been flexed	2	
Quantification of profit difference	2	
Maximum for profit variance		__4__
MAXIMUM FOR TASK		__20__

Suggested solution

From: Tom Smart TS@FX.co.uk

To: John Howard JH@FX.co.uk

Sent: 7th May 2015, 16.04

Subject: May Variance Statement

Please find an explanation of the variances shown in the statement sent to you on 5th June.

Sales variances

Sales volume contribution variance

You are correct in stating the number of units sold during May was 200 more than was planned, which is why the sales volume contribution variance is favourable. Each additional unit sold should have yielded an additional $90 of contribution. (Contribution is selling price of $250 less material of $100, less labour of $40 less variable overheads of $20.)

However as well as looking at the results for the sales volume variance we also need to think about whether or not each unit actually generated $90 of contribution by examining the sale price and the cost variances.

Sales price variance

The adverse variance has occurred as here we are examining what the actual number of units sold (1,200 units) generated as revenue compared to what was anticipated. The adverse variance here means that the sales price per unit was less than expected.

The interdependence between the sales variances cannot be ignored. It is likely that to sell the additional 200 units the selling price had to be reduced, or a reduction in the selling price stimulated the greater level of demand.

Cost variances

Materials

Each unit was budgeted to need 5 kg of material at a cost of $20 per kg. The variance report shows an adverse materials price variance of $6,300 and an adverse materials usage variance of $6,000.

This means that each unit needed more than 5 kg of material and the cost per kg was more than the budgeted $20.

FX's reputation for quality is closely linked to the quality of materials used in production. Adverse material price variances could be due to the need to purchase higher quality inputs in light of concerns about returned products.

Adverse material price variances could be due to price increases within the market generally or careless purchasing decisions. Adverse material usage variances could be due to defective material, excessive waste, theft, or even stricter quality control, to maintain production standards.

Note that the price and usage variance may be interrelated. For example, if material had been purchased and used and was subsequently found to be defective, then better quality material would have to be purchased (presumably at a price higher than the standard) and the units re-worked. This would lead to adverse price and usage variances.

Labour Rate variance

Each unit was budgeted to need 4 hours of labour at a cost of $10 per hour. The variance report shows a favourable labour rate variance and an adverse labour efficiency variance.

This means that each unit needed more than 4 hours of labour but the cost per hour was less than the budgeted $10 per hour.

A favourable labour rate variance may be due to the use of apprentices or other workers at a rate of pay lower than standard.

Labour Efficiency variance

An adverse labour efficiency variance may be due to lack of staff training or experience, use of sub-standard material or errors in allocating time to jobs.

Note that inexperienced workers will probably be paid at a lower rate so the adverse efficiency and favourable rate variance may be interrelated.

Variable overheads

Each unit was budgeted to need 4 hours at a cost of $5 per hour. The variance report shows no expenditure variance but an adverse efficiency variance of $1,200.

This means that each unit needed more than 4 hours but the budgeted cost of $5 per hour was the same as the actual cost per hour.

The reasons for an adverse variable efficiency variance are the same as those of the adverse labour efficiency variance above (because the variance overhead absorption rate is based on direct labour hours.)

Fixed overheads

The budgeted fixed overhead amount was $70,000 per month. The $4,000 adverse variance on the variance report tells us that the actual cost was $74,000 for May instead of the budgeted amount.

Profit variance

The budgeted profit on the variance report has been 'flexed' (adjusted) to account for the fact that 1,200 units were sold instead of 1,000. Using all the budgeted costs and income per unit, 1,200 units should have made a profit of $38,000. Because of the variances mentioned above, the actual profit was $11,140, ie $26,860 lower than it should have been.

Please let me know if I can help you further.

Kind regards,

Tom

Competency coverage

Sub-task	Technical		Business acumen	People		Leadership		Max
	Variances	16						16
	Profit	4						4
Total		**20**						**20**

Variances should be very familiar to all students, the focus here was on explanation of the likely causes of variances taking into account the "big picture" and the information from the scenario. Sub-task 1 requires students to identify potential causes for variances which have already been calculated and recognise interdependencies. As this information is not being used to make decisions all of the marks will fall into the technical competence.

Task 2

Suggested solution

From: Sophie Best SB@RDF.co.uk

To: Rachel Fisher RF@RDF.co.uk

Sent: 8th June 2015, 11.12 a.m.

Subject: Chart

Rachel,

The chart prepared is what is known as a breakeven chart. It demonstrates visually the number of services which must be sold in order to breakeven. Breaking even means that the company will cover all of its costs (both fixed and variable). Below this level the company would make a loss and beyond it a profit. Looking at and being aware of the breakeven point should be a good starting point for avoiding a loss.

The x axis shows the value of the sales revenue and the y axis shows the corresponding level of profit (or loss). The graph begins with a loss of £20,000. This is because even if RDF did not provide any services it would still incur the fixed costs of £20,000.

There are two breakeven points shown on the graph, both are valid but based on different assumptions about the mix of services provided.

Point A is RDF's breakeven point on the assumption that the services are sold in order of their profitability per £ of sales. (This is known as the c/s ratio - a calculation which is used to rank the products according to how much contribution they make per £ of sales). Service K has the highest c/s ratio (of 55.5% - this means that every £1 of sales of service K results in 55.5p of contribution towards fixed costs) and so would be assumed to be provided first, followed by service L and so on until the breakeven sales value is reached.

Point B is the average breakeven point for RDF working on the assumption that services are provided in the ratio 1,000:2,300:1,450:1,970 (ie the budgeted proportions until the breakeven sales value is reached). This is known as the constant mix.

You can see that the breakeven point is higher – nearly £60,000 of sales are required to breakeven if sales are sold in the constant mix. This is because it is an average and uses a weighted average contribution figure. This is more realistic than the breakeven point at A, because RDF needs to provide all of the services to keep customers satisfied.

Limitations of using breakeven analysis:

Although it is a useful starting point for working out the minimum sales revenue and/or services that must be sold to cover total costs, it is based on a number of assumptions which form the basis of its limitations:

It is assumed that units are sold in a constant mix. This is unlikely to be the case in reality as the proportion of services which are sold is affected by lots of factors beyond our control. For example, there may be seasonal fluctuations in the demand for the services or demand may be affected by the availability of substitute services, changing prices or consumer tastes.

It is also assumed that all costs and revenues are constant. However, there may be a need to offer some services at a reduced price, eg for important clients. In reality costs are rarely constant either.

Please let me know if you have any questions or need any further information.

Kind regards,

Sophie

Accountant

RDF

Competency coverage

Sub-task	Technical		Business acumen		People		Leadership		M
	Explanation of graph	5							
	Explanation of points A&B	6							
	Limitations	4							
Total		15							

Students should be able to interpret and explain graphs and the terminology used in breakeven analysis to non-accountants. As this requirement does not involve making a decision all of the marks will fall into the technical competence.

People skills marks might be available in scenarios such as this one, where the audience has very limited financial knowledge.

Task 3

Marking scheme	Marks	Marks
Impact of material shortages		
Definition of Principle Budget Factor	1	
Each impact (1 mark if identified, 2 if explained)	4	
Maximum for impact		<u>5</u>
Using ZBB		
Issues with incremental budgeting (1 mark each)	2	
Definition of ZBB	2	
Benefits of using ZBB (1 mark each)	2	
Maximum ZBB		<u>5</u>
Problems of preparing forecasts		
Predicting future	1	
Effect of competition	1	
Random variations	1	
External changes (eg political, economic, environmental, technological, social)	2	
Maximum for problems		<u>5</u>
Maximum for task		<u>15</u>

Suggested solution

Report to Mr Watts and Mr Austen

Re: Budgeting

Purpose of Report:

This report will cover the following:

- The impact that a shortage of material AP could have on budget preparation and other areas of BR

- Using ZBB to overcome some of the problems of incremental budgeting

- The general problems of preparing forecasts as the basis for the budgetary plan

The impact of a shortage of Material AP

If Material AP is in short supply during the year it will be referred to as the principal budget factor, key or limiting budget factor.

This means that it is the factor that limits the activities of the organisation. The scarcity of material AP will mean that there is a limit to how many units can be produced and ultimately sold.

The company could try to obtain alternative supplies or substitute products. If this is not possible, the impact this will have is that production will be limited by the supply of material AP and therefore, once this has been identified, the production budget has to be prepared before all others.

In addition, to make use of limited resources the company will have to concentrate production on the product that maximises contribution per limiting factor.

Issues with using Incremental budgeting

Incremental budgeting is based on the previous period's budget, adjusted for current period changes – for example, BR's material purchases budget was increased by 4% to account for inflation of material prices.

The main disadvantage of incremental budgeting is that any inefficiencies in the previous year's budget remain in the current year. Any budgetary slack already built into the budget will be maintained. This can lead to wasteful spending.

Using Zero based budgeting (ZBB)

(ZBB) builds the budget from zero and justifies each item of cost from scratch. This will require detailed analysis of BR's activities, and leads to the identification of inefficient activities, thus preventing the inclusion of budgetary slack. It should also encourage more efficient spending – ie only on activities that have been fully justified.

Furthermore, by forcing a detailed budget review, ZBB will help BR by better reflecting the changing external environment. This is especially important as competition increases and external factors become more important as the current use of incremental budgeting is very inward-looking and unresponsive to external factors.

Forecasting problems

All forecasts are subject to error, but the likely errors vary from case to case.

- The further into the future the forecast is for, the more unreliable it is likely to be, particularly since BR is facing increased competition.

- The less data available on which to base the forecast, the less reliable the forecast.

- The pattern of trend and seasonal variations may not continue in the future.

- Random variations may upset the pattern of trend and seasonal variation.

There are a number of changes that may also make it difficult for BR to forecast future events.

• Political and economic changes	Changes in interest rates, exchange rates or inflation can mean that future sales and costs are difficult to forecast. In particular the restricted supply of BR's specialised materials might cause rapid cost inflation.
• Environmental changes	Global warming and milder winters in the UK might affect the demand for BR's insulating products.
• Technological changes	These may mean that the past is not a reliable indication of likely future events. New and improved insulating products developed by competitors might erode the demand for BR's products.
• Social changes	Alterations in taste, fashion and the social acceptability of products can cause forecasting difficulties.

Competency coverage

Sub-task	Technical		Business acumen	People		Leadership		Max
	Impact of material shortages	5						5
	Using ZBB	5						5
	Problems preparing forecasts	5						5
Total		15						15

Students should be aware of both the need to attempt to prepare forecasts and the problems inherent in doing so. As this requirement does not required a decision to be made all of the marks will fall into the technical competence.

Task 4

Marking scheme	Marks	Marks
advantages & disadvantages of involving partners		
Advantages – 1 mark each if listed, 2 if explained	Max 6	
Disadvantages – 1 mark each if listed, 2 if explained	Max 6	
Maximum		12
feedback and feedforward control		
Definition feedback	1	
Definition feedforward	1	
Examples – max 2 marks for each example	4	
Maximum		6
MAXIMUM FOR TASK		18

Suggested solution

> From: Lee Ridley LR@law.co.uk
>
> To: Phil Webster PW@law.co.uk
>
> Sent: 9th June 2015, 11.12 a.m.
>
> Subject: Budgeting ad control
>
> Phil,
>
> <u>Advantages of participation</u>
>
> There are several reasons why it is a good idea to involve the other partners in the budget setting process. The main potential benefit is greater transparency which will help to further partners' knowledge of the budgeting system. Each partner will understand exactly which targets they are responsible for and how performance in each area will be measured.
>
> The partners will also understand how elements of the budget are interdependent. For example, if actual fee income is significantly below budget, it is unlikely that cash targets will be met.
>
> Involving the partners should also improve the accuracy of the budgets as they are the people with detailed knowledge of market conditions and they should be aware of any changes which could impact on the budget.
>
> Overall the combination of all of these factors should mean that the partners will be more motivated to achieve the budgets as they have been involved in setting them.

Disadvantages of participation

A potentially adverse consequence of involving the other partners in the budget setting process is that poor attitudes or hostile behaviour may be shown towards the budgetary control system.

Partners may feel pressured by the draft budget and may complain that it is not realistic. They may attempt to build slack into the budget to ensure that targets are more easily achievable than if the budget was set solely by you and this could lead to the firm becoming less efficient in the long-term.

Feedback control

A feedback control system can be defined as the process of reporting back control information to management and the control of information itself. In a business, it is information produced from within the organisation (management control reports) with the purpose of helping management and other employees with control decisions.

In a firm of solicitors, a partner may explain that the reason for actual fee income being significantly above budget is due to the win of a new client. As a result of this feedback, the central budget may be updated to take account of the increased fee income in the future.

Feedforward control

A feedforward control system is a system which aims to forecast differences between actual and planned outcomes and implement action, before the event, to avoid such differences.

An example would be the comparison of the original cash budget (taking the overdraft facility into account) with the target cash balance. Planned expenditure may have to be postponed in order to ensure that the solicitors meet cash targets and stay within the limits of the overdraft facility. In such instance, a second draft of the cash budget will be prepared.

I hope that this helps, please contact me if you require further clarification.

Kind regards,

Lee

Competency coverage

Sub-task	Technical		Business acumen		People		Leadership		Max
	Involving partners in budget setting	12							12
	Feedback & feedforward	6							6
Total		18							18

It is important to appreciate the links between the budget setting process and motivation. As this requirement does not involve making a decision all of the marks will fall into the technical competence.

Task 5

Marking scheme	Marks

traditional AC v ABC

The various support activities that are involved in making products   or providing services are identified

ABC recognises that there are many different drivers of cost not just production or sales volume

The cost drivers are identified in order to recognise a causal link between activities and costs

They are then used as the basis to attach activity costs to a particular product or service.

Maximum

2 marks per valid point

Max 6

benefits of ABC

 Cost drivers identified provide information to management to enable them to improve profitability

Cost driver analysis provides information to management on how costs can be controlled and managed

Variance analysis will also be more useful as it is based on more accurate product costs

The establishment of more accurate product costs should also help managers to assess product profitability and make better decisions concerning pricing and product mix

Maximum

Maximum for task

1 mark per benefit

1 mark for further explanation or example

$\frac{6}{}$

$\frac{12}{}$

Suggested solution

From: Kate Jones KJ@GH.co.uk

To: Harry West HW@GH.co.uk

Sent: 25th May 20X5, 9.03 a.m.

Subject: Costing

How ABC differs from a traditional absorption costing system

The key difference between an ABC system and an absorption costing system is the way in which the fixed overhead cost is included within the standard cost of a boat. It is important to note that the treatment of direct material, direct labour and variable overheads are the same in both.

At the moment, under absorption costing, total fixed overheads and total machine hours are estimated at the start of the year and these are used to calculate an overhead absorption rate for fixed overheads on a machine hours basis. Therefore we are assuming that there is a direct link between the overhead being incurred and the amount of machine hours worked on each product. In other words we are assuming that production overhead costs are driven by machine hours.

Under ABC, instead of assuming that overhead costs are driven by machine hours, there is an assumption that costs are driven by activities which are known as cost drivers. For each activity or cost driver there will be a cost pool which is simply the total overhead cost generated by that activity.

Benefits of introducing ABC system

1. ### Increased accuracy of costs

   The current method of absorption costing allows overheads to be related to the speedboat types in a rather arbitrary way. This means that the overhead costs attributed to each procedure will not be particularly accurate. ABC focuses on what causes costs to increase (the cost drivers). For example, ABC has identified the various main activities of machining, set-up, quality inspection and stores issue and receipt and what drives the costs for these activities. This establishes a more accurate overhead cost per speedboat type.

2. ### Profitability and cost control

   The company will be able to assess the profitability of each speedboat type more realistically. ABC facilitates a good understanding of what drives overhead costs and so the profitability calculation of each procedure is more accurate. More accurate costs and knowledge of what drives them provide the company with information which may be used to control or reduce costs and therefore improve profitability.

3. ### Pricing and market position

   Using ABC shows that the Ultra speedboat is even less profitable than first thought (12.5% gross profit instead of 16.1%) and that the Deluxe speedboat is the most profitable (25.6% gross profit). The company could consider increasing the price for the Ultra although this would depend on the current market prices and whether the price increase would affect the company's market position.

   The company could also consider the possibility of no longer producing the Ultra speedboat and instead producing some other more profitable speedboat, or more of the Deluxe speedboat if there is sufficient demand.

4. ### Activity based management

   The use of ABC can encourage an activity based management system. ABM applications include the identification of value added and non-value added processes. Efficiency is measured through cost driver rates.

I hope that this helps, please ask if you need further information.

Kind regards,

Kate

Competency coverage

Sub-task	Technical		Business acumen		People		Leadership		M
	Differences	6							
	Benefits	6							
Total		12							1

Students should appreciate that ABC is a form of AC, but the differences and the additional information make it more meaningful for decision making. As this information is not being used to make decisions all of the marks will fall into the technical competence.

Task 6

Marking scheme	Marks	Marks
Explanation of figures & EV		
Demand	2	
Supply	2	
Supply caps contribution available	2	
Maximum		6
Recommendation		
10 maximin	2	
11 EV	2	
12 maximax	2	
Final conclusion – decision	2	
Maximum		8
MAXIMUM FOR TASK		14

Suggested solution

From: Annie Holmes AH@PB.co.uk

To: Paul Berry PB@PB.co.uk

Sent: 25th May 20X5, 9.13 a.m.

Subject: Production levels

Explanation of figures in Payoff Table:

The nine values shown here are the amounts of profit that would be generated if production levels were set at 10, 11 or 12 combined with demand. The company can control production, but not demand. The reason why the contribution generated by producing 10 batches is £500 regardless of external demand is because if we have only made 10 batches we only have 10 batches to sell.

The same is true if we produce 11 batches, it doesn't matter if external demand is 11 or 12 we will still only have 11 batches of bread to sell. It is only at a production level of 12 that all predicted external demand can be satisfied.

The "best" outcome in this table refers to the highest possible profit that could be earned from this production level and this is why the table shows 12 as having the "best" outcome, because there is a chance that profit of £600 could be generated. It does not however, quantify the probability of this occurring, so for this reason I also prepared the EV Table.

Explanation of EV table

The second table I sent applies the probabilities of the different demand levels occurring. Our sales records show that there is a 30% chance that 10 batches will be demanded, 50% chance of 11 batches and 20% chance of 12 batches. This means that although the contribution to profit would be greatest if 12 batches were made and sold, there is only a 20% chance that all 12 would actually be sold.

The calculation of an expected value (EV) produces a weighted average result of all possible outcomes, where each outcome is weighted by the probability of its occurrence. This is a valuable measure where outcomes will occur many times over, such as the number of customers arriving each day over a period of three months.

Recommendation for South Bakery

There is no one universally correct decision about how many loaves to produce – instead the decision should be tailored depending on attitude to risk. I have presented a summary of the options:

Choose to make 10 batches – this is based upon the maximin basis. The maximin basis is short for 'maximising the minimum possible outcome'. This means that the decision maker will select the option that has the **best outcome even if the worst situation arises**. 10 batches would be chosen because the minimum contribution would be £500. This is a risk averse approach to decision making as it limits the potential upside too as £500 is also the maximum contribution.

The other thing to bear in mind if 10 batches are made is what might happen to customers who arrive once all of the bread has been sold – there is what we call an opportunity cost and they may go elsewhere for their bread. This is challenging to quantify.

Choose to make 11 batches – this would be chosen based upon EVs, as the highest long run average contribution to profit is £529. Although this does not correspond to an actual possible profit outcome it is a long run average expected to occur over time. This is the risk neutral approach to decision making.

Choose to make 12 batches – this is based on the maximax attitude to decision making, or a risk seeker's approach. Despite there only being a 20% chance of profits being £600, choosing 12 batches means that you are prepared to gamble on demand being 12 because of the higher potential profits.

Recommendation

As you asked for a recommendation I would suggest that we make 11 batches per day, some days there might be waste, but over the year the contribution to profits from artisan breads in the south bakery should be higher than if 10 or 12 batches are produced daily.

I hope that this helps, please ask if you need further information.

Kind regards,

Annie

Competency coverage

Sub-task	Technical		Business acumen		People		Leadership		Max
	Explanation of figures	6							6
	Recommendation – 3 attitudes	6			Decision-making	2			8
Total		12				2			14

It is important to recognise that although businesses do not have a crystal ball we need to attempt to take into consideration the likelihood of an event occurring and use that when making decisions. Students should be able to apply attitudes to risk to offer advice when decisions are being made. The people skills marks were given for the ability to make decisions in the specific context of the information in the scenario about attitudes to risk.

Topic 4 – P1 Further Tasks

Task 7 - RFT

(indicative timing : 30 mins)

RFT is an engineering company and you, Jeff Jones, as management accountant, have been asked to provide a quotation for a contract to build a new engine. The potential customer is not a current customer of RFT, but the directors of RFT are keen to try and win the contract as they believe that this may lead to more contracts in the future. As a result you intend to price the contract using relevant costs.

The following information has been obtained from a two-hour meeting that the Production Director of RFT had with the potential customer.

Exhibit 1

The Production Director is paid an annual salary equivalent to $1,200 per 8-hour day.

110 square metres of material A will be required. This is a material that is regularly used by RFT and there are 200 square metres currently in inventory. These were bought at a cost of $12 per square metre. They have a resale value of $10.50 per square metre and their current replacement cost is $12.50 per square metre.

30 litres of material B will be required. This material will have to be purchased for the contract because it is not otherwise used by RFT. The minimum order quantity from the supplier is 40 litres at a cost of $9 per litre. RFT does not expect to have any use for any of this material that remains after this contract is completed.

Components costing $3,000 (= $50 × 60 components) will be required from company HY. HY is another company in the same group as RFT.

A total of 235 direct labour hours will be required. The current wage rate for the appropriate grade of direct labour is $11 per hour. Currently RFT has 75 direct labour hours of spare capacity at this grade that is being paid under a guaranteed wage agreement. The additional hours would need to be obtained by either (i) overtime at a total cost of $14 per hour; or (ii) recruiting temporary staff at a cost of $12 per hour. However, if temporary staff are used they will not be as experienced as RFT's existing workers and will require 10 hours supervision by an existing supervisor who would be paid overtime at a cost of $18 per hour for this work.

25 machine hours will be required. The machine to be used is already leased for a weekly leasing cost of $600. It has a capacity of 40 hours per week. The machine has sufficient available capacity for the contract to be completed. The variable running cost of the machine is $7 per hour.

The company absorbs its fixed overhead costs using an absorption rate of $20 per direct labour hour.

You send an email to your boss, Jane Rice with the following cost schedule, as a basis to be used for the quotation:

Exhibit 2

Cost item	$
Production Director's time	Nil
Material A	1,375
Material B	360
Components from supplier HY	3,000
Direct labour (160 × $12)+(10 × $18)	2,100
Machine costs (25 × $7)	175
Fixed overheads	Nil
Total relevant cost	7,010

Upon receipt of your cost schedule, Jane sends you the following email:

From: Jane Rice JR@RFT.com

To: Jeff Jones JJ@RFT.com

Sent: 16th August 20X5, 10.08 am

Subject: Quote using relevant costs

Jeff,

Thank you for the cost quote that you sent me. I have to admit that I know very little about relevant costing and the basis of your calculations.

It would be very useful for me if you could send me an email that explains the following.

What is the meaning of relevant cost?

Why is the production director's time $nil?

Why is the material A cost $12.50 x 110 instead of $12 x 110?

Is there an error in the material B calculation? (30 litres x $9 = $270, not $360 giving a difference of $90)

Why are only 160 hours of labour paid for?

Why are the leasing costs of $600 not included in the figure for machine costs?

Why are fixed overhead costs $nil?

As you may know, each component from HY is being transferred to RFT taking account of HY's opportunity cost of the component. The variable cost that will be incurred by HY is $28 per component.

What are the factors that would be considered by HY to determine the opportunity cost of the component?

Kind regards,

Jane Rice (MD)

Write your response to the email from Jane

Task 8 - DE

(indicative timing : 35 mins)

You are Lee Jones, a management accountant. DE is a distributor of three models of Tablet PCs (Premium, Deluxe and Superfast) to retailers and uses a marginal costing system. The company was set up several years ago by two colleagues (Doug Sharma and Ed Chung) who had worked together previously. Ed dealt with the financial side of the DE business but retired from the company at the beginning of August. You have been appointed as the management accountant as Doug is busy managing the sales department and has little experience of finance.

The details of the sales volume budget, standard selling prices and standard variable costs (produced by Ed) for each model for July were as follows:

Exhibit 1

Sales volume budget

Premium	7,000 units
Deluxe	5,000 units
Superfast	8,000 units

	Premium $ per unit	Deluxe $ per unit	Superfast $ per unit
Standard selling price	400	450	500
Standard variable cost	300	320	350

At the end of July, Ed decided that the impact of the failure of a major competitor had been underestimated and produced a revised sales volume budget as follows:

Exhibit 2

Revised sales volume budget

Premium	9,800 units
Deluxe	7,000 units
Superfast	11,200 units

Actual results for July

	Premium	Deluxe	Superfast
Sales volume (units)	11,000	6,000	9,000
Selling price per unit	$410	$440	$520
Variable cost per unit	$300	$320	$350

When you joined in August, the first thing you did was to produce an operating statement and email it to Doug (**Exhibit 3**). You stated in your email that planning and operational variances provide better information for planning and control purposes.

Exhibit 3

	$ F	$ A	$
Budgeted contribution			2,550,000
Sales quantity contribution planning variances			
Premium	280,000		
Deluxe	260,000		
Superfast	480,000		1,020,000 (F)
Revised budgeted contribution			3,570,000
Sales mix contribution operational variances			
Premium	190,000		
Deluxe		65,000	
Superfast		210,000	85,000 (A)
Sales quantity contribution operational variances			
Premium		70,000	
Deluxe		65,000	
Superfast		120,000	255,000 (A)
Sales price operational variances			
Premium	110,000		
Deluxe		60,000	
Superfast	180,000		230,000 (F)
Actual contribution			3,460,000

Doug has now sent you the following email:

From: Doug Sharma DS@DE.com
To: Lee Jones LJ@DE.com
Sent: 16th August 20X5, 10.08 am
Subject: Operating statement

Lee,

Thank you for the statement you sent me. I have to admit that I know very little about operating statements and the basis of your calculations.

It would be very useful for me if you could send me an email that explains

The meaning of the sales mix contribution variance and sales quantity contribution variance.

Whether they are useful to me.

I think Ed used to produce a sales volume variance calculation so I am surprised that you haven't.

Please could you also explain why planning and operational variances provide better information for planning and control purposes?

I would also like to know why the variances used to reconcile profit in a standard marginal costing system are different from those used in a standard absorption costing system and possible reasons for adverse and favourable fixed overhead variances.

Kind regards,

Doug

Doug Sharma
Managing Director

Write your response to the email from Doug

Task 9 - Noclue Co

(indicative timing : 35 mins)

Noclue Co produces an expensive type of bicycle. The manager, Jo Little, believes that the business is more efficient than ever as they are producing more bicycles in a week than ever before. They are even running out of space in the inventory warehouse. Each employee has a single job within the manufacture of the bicycles and once trained, the employee does not do any other work other than the task they have been trained to do.

The number of bicycles sold over the last 3 years has been as follows.

	20X1	20X2	20X3
Bicycles sold	356	357	340

You are Sam Hughes, and you have recently been employed by Noclue Co as a management accountant. **Today is 1 March 20X4.** One of your friends sends you an internet link to a customer review website of bicycles. An extract is shown below.

Exhibit 1

Review of Noclue bike ZA1 2 Jan 20X4

Very disappointed with this bike. There were mechanical problems from day 1. I asked for a refund.

Review of Noclue bike BS3 4 Feb 20X4

Took this bike back to be repaired within a month of having bought it!

Review of Noclue bike ZA1 26 Dec 20X3

My son was very upset with the low quality of this bike.

Review of Noclue bike BS3 2 Dec 20X3

Delay in receipt of my customised bike due to staff sickness

You decide to have a look at the production and accounting processes and you send an email to Jo Little suggesting that a just-in-time (JIT) system should be used. You say that JIT has financial benefits and that a total quality management (TQM) system is important within a JIT system.

Upon receipt of your email, Jo Little sends you the following email:

From: Jo Little JL@NC.com

To: Sam Hughes SH@NC.com

Sent: 16th March 20X4, 10.08 am

Subject: JIT and TQM

Hi Sam,

Thank you for the email you sent me. I have tried to read up a little on JIT and TQM since receiving your email, however, I still have a lot of questions. I have been very happy with the process that we have been using as we have produced more bicycles per week this year than ever before.

It would be very useful for me if you could send me an email that explains

Five key features of a JIT production system.

The financial benefits of JIT.

Three key features of TQM

Four reasons why the adoption of TQM is particularly important within a JIT production environment.

Kind regards,

Jo Little
Managing Director

Write your response to Jo Little

Task 10 - JRL

(indicative timing : 35 mins)

You are Fred Seeraj and you have recently been appointed management accountant at a company called JRL. JRL is a small company that makes car parts. It manufactures two car parts, J and L, from different combinations of the same resources.

The maximum weekly demand for parts J and L is 400 units and 450 units respectively and this is the normal weekly production volume achieved by JRL.

However, the production manager, Trishni, has just forwarded you an email which she has received from the suppliers.

Exhibit 1

From: Trishni Jones TJ@JRL.com

To: Fred Seeraj FS@JRL.com

Sent: 16th August 20X5, 10.30 am

Fred – please see below.

From: Andy Sharma AS@suppliers.com

To: Trishni Jones TJ@JRL.com

Sent: 16th August 20X5, 10.08 am

Subject: Supplies after natural disaster

Dear Trishni,

I am sorry to inform you that because of the natural disaster in Northland, we will be unable to completely fulfil your materials order. For the next four weeks material A will be limited to 900kg and material B will be limited to 1,750kg.

I apologise for the inconvenience but I'm sure you understand that the situation is out of our control.

Kind regards

Andy

Unfortunately this coincides with a shortage of labour hours due to sickness and a shortage of machine hours due to a machine breakdown. The labour shortage, however, is not a limiting factor. These shortages are expected to be back to normal in 4 weeks.

You decide to produce a graph using linear programming and you quickly send it to the managing director, Alison, without a full explanation. You state in the email that the shadow price of labour is $nil and the shadow price of material A is $11.70.

Exhibit 2

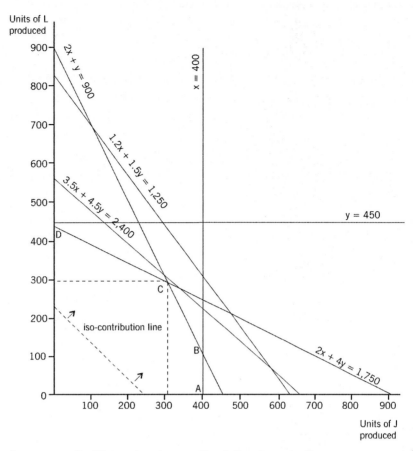

Upon receipt of your email, Alison sends you the following email:

From: Alison Gill AG@JRL.com
To: Fred Seeraj FS@JRL.com
Sent: 16th August 20X5, 10.08 am
Subject: Linear programming

Hi Fred,

Thank you for the graph that you sent me. It looks very impressive! I have to admit that I know very little about linear programming and the basis of your calculations and what it all means.

It would be very useful for me if you could send me an email that explains

Why you used the graphical method. I have heard there is a something called a simplex method.

What the graph is telling me.

The meaning of the points OABCD and the iso contribution line.

What the relevance of the shadow price figures are.

How you would calculate by how much the selling price of J could increase before the optimal solution would change.

Kind regards,

Alison

Write your response to the email from Alison

Task 11 - Risk Away Co

(indicative timing 35 mins)

Risk Away Co is a company which makes different types of chocolate bars and boxes of chocolates. You are Ola Mars and you have recently been appointed management accountant. The managing director, Jo Wispa, has told you about three marketing campaigns. Jo wants to invest in one of the three campaigns. They all have a life of five years and no residual value. You evaluate the marketing campaigns taking into consideration the range of possible outcomes that could result from the investment.

You send a summary to Jo.

Exhibit 1			
Marketing campaign			
	J	*K*	*L*
	$	$	$
Expected net present value	400,000	800,000	400,000
Standard deviation of net present value	35,000	105,000	105,000

Upon receipt of your email, Jo sends you the following email:

From: Jo Wispa JW@RA.com
To: Ola Mars OM@RA.com

Ola,

Thank you for the schedule of data that you sent me. I have to admit that I know very little about expected values, standard deviation and the basis of your calculations.

It would be very useful for me if you could send me an email that explains the following.

The meaning of the data in your schedule

How it may be used by us when choosing between alternative campaigns

I have had a quick look on the internet for information about expected values and wonder if you could also explain:

Why the use of expected values might not be a satisfactory way of dealing with uncertainty in a once-only decision

Why a risk averse decision maker might use the maximin basis to make a choice between options where the outcome is uncertain

How the value of perfect information is calculated.

I have also read that 'Decision rules based on expected values assume that the decision maker is risk neutral'. Please could you explain this?

Kind regards,

Jo Wispa (MD)

Write your response to the email from Jo

Task 12 - WTL

(indicative timings : 35 mins)

You are Jatty Jones, the new management accountant at WTL. WTL manufactures and sells four products: W, X, Y, and Z from a single factory and factory shop. Sales of each product are independent of each other. Each of the products is manufactured in batches of 100 units using a just-in-time manufacturing process and consequently there is no inventory of any product. This batch size of 100 units cannot be altered without significant cost implications. Although the products are manufactured in batches of 100 units, they are sold as single units at the market price. WTL has a significant number of competitors and is forced to accept the market price for each of its products.

The managing director, Ketan Shah, is currently reviewing the profit it makes from each product, and for the business as a whole, and has produced a profit statement for the latest period:

Product	W	X	Y	Z	Total
Number of:					
Units sold	100,000	130,000	80,000	150,000	
Machine hours	200,000	195,000	80,000	300,000	775,000
Direct labour hours	50,000	130,000	80,000	75,000	335,000

Product	W	X	Y	Z	Total
	$	$	$	$	$
Sales	1,300,000	2,260,000	2,120,000	1,600,000	7,280,000
Direct materials	300,000	910,000	940,000	500,000	2,650,000
Direct labour	400,000	1,040,000	640,000	600,000	2,680,000
Overhead costs	400,000	390,000	160,000	600,000	1,550,000
Profit /(Loss)	200,000	(80,000)	380,000	(100,000)	400,000

Note

1   The overhead costs have been absorbed into the above product costs using an absorption rate of $2 per machine hour.

2   Further analysis of the overhead cost shows that some of it is caused by the number of machine hours used, some is caused by the number of batches produced and some of the costs are product specific fixed overheads that would be avoided if the product were discontinued. Other general fixed overhead costs would be avoided only by the closure of the factory. Details of this analysis are as follows:

	$'000	$'000
Machine hour related		310
Batch related		230
Product specific fixed overhead:		
Product W	500	
Product X	50	
Product Y	100	
Product Z	50	700
General fixed overhead		310
		1,550

Mr Shah is concerned that two of its products are loss making and has carried out an analysis of its products and costs and expresses his concern to you, the new management accountant.

You are unhappy about the way in which the profit statement has been prepared, particularly the overhead figures. It seems that relevant costs haven't been used. You prepare a revised statement and email it to Mr Shah saying that your statement is more suitable for decision making.

Exhibit 1

Columnar statement for WTL

	W	X	Y	Z	Total
	$'000	$'000	$'000	$'000	$'000
Sales	1,300	2,260	2,120	1,600	7,280
Variable costs:					
Direct materials	(300)	(910)	(940)	(500)	(2,650)
Direct labour	(400)	(1,040)	(640)	(600)	(2,680)
Overheads:					
Machine-hour-related overhead	(80)	(78)	(32)	(120)	(310)
Batch-related overhead	(50)	(65)	(40)	(75)	(230)
Gross contribution	470	167	468	305	1,410
Directly attributable fixed costs	(500)		(100)	(50)	(700)
		(50)			
Net contribution	(30)	117	368	255	710
General fixed costs					(310)
Overall profit					400

Upon receipt of your email, Mr Shah sends you the following response:

From: Ketan Shah KS@WTL.com

To: Jatty Jones JJ@WTL.com

Sent: 16th August 20X5, 10.08 am

Subject: Profit statement

Jatty,

Thank you for the statement you sent me. I have to admit that I don't quite understand why you have revised my profit statement. It would be very useful for me if you could send me an email that explains:

Why your statement is suitable for decision making

Advises which, if any, of our four products should be discontinued in order to maximise our profits.

I have recently read that activity-based costing can be used in a retail environment such as our factory shop. Please could you explain how activity-based costing can be used in a retail environment to improve our decision-making and profitability?

Kind regards,

Ketan Shah (MD)

Write your response to the email from Mr Shah

Topic 4 – P1 Further Tasks Solutions

Task 7

Marking scheme

	Marks	Marks
Relevant costs		
Meaning of relevant cost	1	
Production director is a past cost	1	
Material A at replacement cost as it is in continual use	1	
Material B at purchase cost as it needs to be bought	1	
Material B min order quantity relevant because there is no other use	1	
Labour. Spare capacity so relevant cost = 160 hours	1	
Labour cost is cheaper of two options	1	
Fixed overheads. Not incremental	1	
Clear layout of email	1	
		9
Opportunity cost		
Identify two factors: capacity & unsatisfied demand	2	
Explain capacity issue (spare = variable cost, full = opportunity cost)	Up to 2	
Explain unsatisfied demand issue (ie opportunity cost)	Up to 2	
	Maximum	6
MAXIMUM FOR TASK		15

Suggested solution

From: Jeff Jones JJ@RFT.com

To: Jane Rice JR@RFT.com

Sent: 25th August 20X5, 9.03 a.m.

Subject: Quote using relevant costs

Dear Jane,

<u>Relevant cost of building the new engine</u>

Relevant costs are costs appropriate to a specific management decision. They are future, incremental cash flows.

The relevant cost of building the new engine is the net incremental cash outflow that will be incurred if the contract is undertaken. Any price in excess of this relevant cost will provide marginal profit for the company.

1   <u>Production Director's time</u>

The cost of the Production Director's time is not relevant for two reasons. The Director is paid a fixed annual salary, and no additional cash expenditure is incurred. The Director's time has already been used, and costs incurred in the past cannot be relevant costs, even if they had resulted in extra cash spending.

Relevant cost = $Nil

2   Material A

If 110 square metres are used from existing inventory, this will lead to additional purchases being required, because the material is in regular use. Therefore, the relevant cost is the current replacement cost

3   Material B

Although only 30 litres of material B are required, the minimum order quantity is 40 litres. The surplus quantity would have no other use and so would presumably be disposed of (a zero cost of disposal is assumed.)

4   Components

The purchase cost is a relevant cost.

5   Direct labour

235 direct labour hours are required. The first 75 hours of direct labour can be obtained at no extra cost, because there is spare capacity for this amount of time, and the employees will be paid anyway under the guaranteed wage agreement.

Therefore, only 160 hours will have to be paid for. These hours can be obtained by getting employees to work overtime, and the incremental cost would be 160 hours × \$14 = \$2,240. Alternatively temporary staff could be used with supervision and the incremental cost would be (160 hours × \$12) + (10 hours × \$18) = \$2,100. The supervisor's time is an incremental cost because it would be overtime work.

Using temporary staff would cost less, and it is assumed that the cheaper option will be selected.

6   Machine costs

The lease cost is a committed cost that will be incurred anyway – it is not a relevant cost. The relevant cost is the incremental cost of using the machine.

7   Fixed overheads

Absorbed fixed overheads are not an incremental cost. It is assumed that there will be no incremental fixed costs as a consequence of performing the contract.

Relevant cost = \$Nil

Opportunity cost

Opportunity cost is the benefit forgone by using a resource for one purpose instead of using it for its most profitable alternative purpose. HY will transfer components to us for \$50 each and the variable cost of making each unit will be \$28. This suggests that the opportunity cost that HY will cover in the transfer price is \$22 per unit.

The following factors should be considered by HY to determine the opportunity cost of the component.

External market sales

It is not clear as to whether there is an external market for the components manufactured by HY. HY may be unable to meet any external market demand as a result of supplying RFT with components. Furthermore, the external market price may be significantly higher than the current transfer price of \$50.

If this is the case, the opportunity cost for HJ would be the maximum contribution forgone as a result of transferring internally rather than selling goods externally.

Raw materials

An opportunity cost can also arise when resources are in short supply.

The shortage of resources in HY may be the raw materials that are used to make the components. If so, making components for RFT would mean producing lower quantities of other components or products, and the opportunity cost would be the contribution forgone from the lost sales of the other items.

Labour time

Similarly, the shortage of resources in HY may be labour time. If labour is in limited supply, producing components for RFT would mean that fewer units of other products or components could be made, and the opportunity cost for HY would be the contribution forgone from lost sales of the other items.

I hope that this helps.

Kind regards,

Jeff

Competency coverage

Sub-task	Technical		Business acumen		People		Leadership		Max
1	Relevant costs	9							9
2	Opportunity cost	6							6
Total		15							15

CIMA P1 does not require competency in business acumen or leadership. People skills are only required for P1 in the form of decision making. The competency required for this question is therefore entirely technical, falling under the heading of core accounting and finance skills.

Task 8

Marking scheme

	Marks	Marks
Sales volume, mix and quantity variance		
1 mark for each valid point	6	
		6
Planning and operational variances		
1-2 marks per valid point	Up to 6	
		6
Fixed overhead variances		
Treatment of fixed costs	Up to 2	
Profit/contribution	Up to 2	
		4
Reasons for fixed overhead variances		
1 mark for each valid point	Up to 4	
		4
MAXIMUM FOR TASK		20

Suggested solution

From: Lee Jones LJ@DE.com

To: Doug Sharma DS@DE.com

Sent: 25th August 20X5, 9.03 a.m.

Subject: Operating statement

Dear Doug,

The sales volume variance, which Ed previously provided, measures the increase or decrease in the standard profit or contribution as a result of the sales volume being higher or lower than budgeted. It is calculated as the difference between actual sales units and budgeted sales units, multiplied by the standard profit per unit When a company sells more than one product, as we do, the sales volume variance can be split into a sales mix and sales quantity variance.

Sales mix contribution variance

The sales mix contribution variance occurs when the proportions of the products sold are different from those in the budget. Premium sold proportionally more than budgeted. Deluxe and Superfast both sold proportionally less than budgeted. Premium has a lower contribution than Deluxe and Superfast so selling more of Premium and less of Deluxe and Superfast resulted in an adverse variance of $85,000.

Sales quantity contribution variance

The sales quantity contribution variance shows the difference in contribution because of a difference in sales volume from budgeted sales volume.

The adverse variance of $255,000 indicates that if the budgeted sales mix had been maintained and the sales increased by 2,000 units, the increased sales volume would have given an extra contribution of $255,000.

I chose to provide this separation of sales volume variance into mix and quantity variances as I believe that it is useful. It highlights that maximising sales volume may not be as advantageous as increasing the sales of the most profitable mix of products.

Separating variances into planning and operational components

Controllable v uncontrollable

The analysis highlights those variances which are controllable and those which are non-controllable. By analysing the total price variance between planning and operational, we can focus on the underlying causes of the total variances and thus identify the controllable increase in costs which could have been avoided.

Motivation

The sales managers' acceptance of the use of variances for performance measurement, and their motivation, is likely to increase if they know that they will not be held responsible for poor planning and faulty standard setting.

Improved standard setting

The planning and standard setting process should improve. Standards should be more accurate, relevant and appropriate.

Effectiveness of planning process

The planning process can be assessed to decide whether there is anything that could have been realistically foreseen. For example, it may be that the planning stage process failed to anticipate likely market trends. This would probably originally have been classed as poor standard setting when in reality, it could have been controlled at the planning stage.

Differences between marginal and absorption variances

There are two differences between the way that variances are calculated in a marginal costing system and in an absorption costing system.

In marginal costing, fixed costs are not absorbed into product costs and so there are no fixed cost variances to explain any under or over absorption of overheads. There will, therefore, be no fixed overhead volume variance. There will, however, be a fixed overhead expenditure variance which is calculated in exactly the same way as for absorption costing systems.

In marginal costing the sales volume variance in units will be valued at standard contribution margin and called the sales volume contribution variance. In standard absorption costing standard profit is used instead of standard contribution.

Reasons for fixed overhead expenditure variances

As we use a marginal costing system the only possible fixed overhead variance that we may have is the fixed overhead expenditure variance.

A favourable variance could arise if we make savings in the costs incurred, for example by switching our energy supplier. Or we could make more economical use of our services, for example, by turning off lights and machinery when they are not in use.

Conversely, an adverse fixed overhead expenditure variance will arise if we make excessive use of services or prices for our overheads are increased.

Kind regards

Lee

Competency coverage

Sub-task	Technical		Business acumen		People		Leadership		M
1	Sales volume, mix and quantity variances	6							
2	Planning and operational variances	6							
3	Fixed overhead variances	4							
4	Reasons for fixed overhead variances	4							
Total		20							

CIMA P1 does not require competency in business acumen or leadership. People skills are only required for P1 in the form of decision making. The competency required for this question is therefore entirely technical, falling under the heading of core accounting and finance skills.

Task 9

Marking scheme

	Marks	Marks
Five features of JIT production system		
1 mark for each valid point	Up to 5	
		5
Financial benefits of JIT		
1-2 marks per valid point	Up to 5	
		5
3 key features of TQM		
1-2 marks per valid point	Up to 5	
		5
4 reasons why TQM is important in JIT		
1-2 marks per valid point	Up to 5	
		5
MAXIMUM FOR TASK		20

Suggested solution

From: Sam Hughes SH@NC.com

To: Jo Little JL@NC.com

Sent: 25th March 20X4, 9.03 a.m.

Subject: JIT/TQM

Dear Jo,

JIT production systems will include the following features.

Multiskilled workers

In a JIT production environment, production processes must be shortened and simplified. Each product family is made in a workcell based on flowline principles. Workers must therefore be more flexible and adaptable, the cellular approach enabling each operative to operate several machines. Operatives are trained to operate all machines on the line and undertake routine preventative maintenance. This is quite different from the system we are currently using where employees cannot do each other's work. Staff sickness can therefore interrupt the manufacture of a bike.

Close relationships with suppliers

For JIT purchasing to be successful it requires us to have confidence that the supplier will deliver on time and that the supplier will deliver materials of 100% quality, that there will be no rejects, returns and hence no consequent production delays. The reliability of suppliers is of utmost importance and hence we must build up close relationships with our suppliers.

Machine cells

With JIT production, factory layouts must change to reduce movement of workers and products. Material movements between operations are minimised by eliminating space between work stations and grouping machines or workers by product or component instead of by type of work performed. Products can flow from machine to machine without having to wait for the next stage of processing or returning to stores. Lead times and work in progress are thus reduced.

Quality

Quality reduces costs. Quality is assured by designing products and processes with quality in mind, introducing quality awareness programmes and statistical checks on output quality, providing continual worker training and implementing vendor quality assurance programmes to ensure that the correct bicycle is made to the appropriate quality level on the first pass through production.

Set-up time reduction

If an organisation is able to reduce manufacturing lead time it is in a better position to respond quickly to changes in customer demand. Reducing set-up time is one way in which this can be done. Machinery set-ups are non-value-added activities which should be reduced or even eliminated.

Financial benefits

JIT systems have a number of financial benefits.

- Reduction in costs of storing inventory
- Reduction in costs associated with scrap, defective units and reworking
- Reduction in the costs of setting up production runs
- Higher revenues as a result of faster response to customer demands
- Reduction in risk of inventory obsolescence

I note that you are pleased with the number of bicycles that we are able to produce per week. However, sales volumes actually fell last year so we have not increased production levels for the right reasons. We have been producing more bicycles per week and having to pay to store inventory. Our quality also seems to have dropped judging by the number of poor complaints that we have had.

Alternative financial benefits

- Increase in labour productivity due to labour being multiskilled and carrying out preventative maintenance

- Reduction of investment in plant space

- Lower investment in inventory

- Reduction in costs of handling inventory

- Higher revenue as a result of reduction in lost sales following failure to meet delivery dates (because of improved quality)

Key features that are present in any organisation which is focused on TQM

Get it right first time

One of the basic principles of TQM is that the cost of preventing mistakes is less than the cost of correcting them once they occur. Therefore an organisation which is focused on TQM, as I think we should be, should be aiming to get things right first time. Every mistake, delay and misunderstanding directly costs money through wasted time and effort.

Continuous improvement

An organisation which is focused on TQM will believe that it is always possible to improve and so the aim should be to 'get it more right next time.' This means that standards will be changed frequently rather than kept at a historical standard.

Design for quality

A TQM environment aims to get it right first time and this means that quality, not faults, must be designed into our bicycles and operations from the outset. Quality control must happen at the various stages in the process of designing our bicycles. Good quality bicycles also means that customers are more likely to be satisfied and our reviews should improve. If our reviews improve, our sales volume will improve.

TQM in a Just-in-time (JIT) systems environment

- JIT production is a system driven by demand for finished products. Work in progress is only processed through a stage of production when it is needed by the next stage. The result is minimal (or in some cases non-existent) inventories of work in progress and finished goods.

- JIT purchasing seeks to match the usage of materials with the delivery of materials from suppliers. This means that material inventories can be kept at near-zero levels.

Eliminating scrap and defective units

Production management within a JIT environment therefore needs to eliminate scrap and defective units during production and avoid the need for reworking of units. Defects stop the production line, creating rework and possibly resulting in a failure to meet delivery dates (as buffer inventories of work in progress and finished goods are not held). Note that we have had bad reviews because of faulty bicycles and late delivery.

Supplier quality assurance

For JIT purchasing to be successful, we must have confidence that our supplier will deliver on time and will deliver materials of 100% quality, that there will be no rejects, returns and hence no consequent production delays. This confidence can be achieved by adopting supplier quality assurance schemes and stringent procedures for acceptance and inspection of goods inwards, which are integral parts of TQM.

Kind regards

Sam

Competency coverage

Sub-task	Technical		Business acumen		People		Leadership		M
1	JIT production	5							
2	Financial benefits of JIT	5							
3	Features of TQM	5							
4	Reasons why TQM is important in JIT system	5							
Total		20							2

CIMA P1 does not require competency in business acumen or leadership. People skills are only required for P1 in the form of decision making. The competency required for this question is therefore entirely technical, falling under the heading of core accounting and finance skills.

Task 10

Marking scheme

	Marks	Marks
Graphical method v simplex method		
1 mark for each valid point	Up to 2	
		2
Meaning of graph, OABCD, iso contribution line		
Graph -1-2 marks per valid point	Up to 3	
OABCD (feasible region) and iso-contribution line	Up to 5	
		8
Relevance of shadow price figures		
Explanation of shadow price	Up to 2	
Explanation of skilled labour	Up to 2	
Explanation of direct material A	Up to 2	
		6
How to calculate change in selling price		
Explain change in the slope of the iso-contribution line	Up to 2	
Explain the evaluation of the extreme points of the feasible region	Up to 2	
		4
MAXIMUM FOR TASK		20

Suggested solution

From: Fred Seeraj FS@JRL.com

To: Alison Gill AG@JRL.com

Sent: 25th August 20X5, 9.03 a.m.

Subject: Linear programming

Dear Alison

Method used

There are two linear programming techniques. The graphical method is used for problems involving two products. The simplex method is used if the problem involves more than two products. As we only produce two products, I used the graphical approach.

What it means

I prepared the graph in order to calculate the optimum number of units of Part J and Part L for us to produce to maximise contribution and therefore profit, for the next four weeks. I had to take into account the fact that we were constrained by the number of labour hours, machine hours and the limited materials availability.

The graph is telling us that the optimum number is to produce approximately 310 units of J and approximately 280 units of L. This will give us the greatest contribution.

Feasible region and iso contribution

OABCD is the area on the graph known as the "feasible region" which shows all of the possible solutions within the limiting boundaries. In other words, it shows all of the possible combinations of the number of units we could produce using our available materials, labour hours and machine hours.

When we have established what the feasible region is, we need to find which of these solutions is best. We are trying to maximise the contribution. The best solution is going to be at a point on the edge of the feasible region. We find this by drawing an iso contribution line. This is a line drawn on the graph where the contribution is the same all the way along. We then push this line out (and as we push it out from the origin the contribution along the line increases) as far as we can until it is just about to completely leave the feasible region.

The point at which it leaves the feasible region is the optimal point. This is the combination of output that maximises contribution.

Shadow price relevance

A shadow price is the additional contribution created by the availability of one extra unit of a limiting factor at its original cost.

The shadow price for skilled labour is nil because, despite the shortage of skilled labour, other resources are even more scarce and they limit output. Labour is not a limiting factor in the current conditions.

Since material A is a limiting factor, if the availability of material A could be increased by one unit, this would change the optimal plan. The shadow price of $11.70 is the additional contribution that would be earned from another unit of A, and so it is the maximum premium that it would be worthwhile paying, on top of the original cost, to obtain an additional unit of material A.

If the selling price of product J changed then, all other things being equal, the relative contribution from the sale of a unit of J would change. This would mean that the gradient of the iso- contribution line would change.

From the graph, the feasible area for a solution is 0ABCD. Currently the extreme point that the iso-contribution line hits is point C. If the gradient of the iso-contribution line changed, then it could hit one of the other extreme points AB or D instead.

In order to determine by how much the selling price of product J would have to increase in order to change the iso-contribution line in that way, we would calculate the unit contributions of product J which would create a gradient that would cause one of the other extreme points to be chosen in preference to C.

Kind regards

Fred

Competency coverage

Sub-task	Technical		Business acumen		People		Leadership		Max
1	Linear programming graphical v simplex	2							2
2	Meaning of graph, feasible region and iso-contribution line	8							8
3	Shadow price	6							6
4	How to calculate change in selling price	4							4
Total		20							20

CIMA P1 does not require competency in business acumen or leadership. People skills are only required for P1 in the form of decision making. The competency required for this question is therefore entirely technical, falling under the heading of core accounting and finance skills.

Task 11

Marking scheme

	Marks	Marks
Meaning of expected NPV and standard deviation		
1 mark for each valid point	Up to 3	
How to choose between different campaigns		
1-2 marks per valid point	Up to 3	
	Max total	5
Expected value limitations and maximin		
1-2 marks per valid point	Up to 6	
		6
Value of perfect information		
1-2 marks per valid point	Up to 3	
		3
Risk neutral		
1-2 marks per valid point	Up to 6	
		6
MAXIMUM FOR TASK		20

Suggested solution

From: Ola Mars OM@RA.com

To: Jo Wispa JW@RA.com

Sent: 25th August 20X5, 9.03 a.m.

Subject: Marketing campaign

Dear Jo,

Explanation of expected net present value and standard deviation

Expected net present value (ENPV).

This measures the sum of the possible range of outcomes for each campaign multiplied by their probabilities. It does not tell us about the range of values however which would allow us to assess the likelihood of profit or loss.

Standard deviation (SD).

Risk can be measured by the possible range of outcomes around the ENPV of the campaigns. One way of doing this is by calculating the SD of the ENPV. We can then assess the campaigns looking at the riskiness as well as the single measure of ENPV.

How would we use this data to choose between investments?

One way of ranking the three campaigns is to compare their ENPVs and choose the campaign with the highest ENPV. This means that campaign K should be chosen with a ENPV of $800,000. We may be risk averse in which case we would choose a campaign where the SD is smaller. This risk profile would be satisfied by choosing campaign J with a SD of $35,000. A more risk seeking management might opt for a campaign where the SD was higher but the outcomes were also higher. They would opt for campaign K which has a SD of $105,000 but also a higher ENPV. We would not opt for campaign L as the ENPV is lower than campaign K and the SD is higher than campaign J.

Expected values are a weighted average result

The calculation of an expected value (EV) produces a weighted average result of all possible outcomes, where each outcome is weighted by the probability of its occurrence. This is a valuable measure where outcomes will occur many times over, such as the number of customers arriving each day over a period of three months.

The limitation of expected values in a once-only decision

However, the use of expected values is of limited usefulness for a once-only decision, perhaps where the decision is based on the prediction of the number of customers arriving on a particular day. This is because the EV does not take account of the range of possible outcomes that could occur on a particular day. If there is a wide range of possible outcomes then actual outcome could be very different from the EV on a particular day.

Therefore for a once-only decision with a wide range of possible outcomes it is probably preferable to apply other techniques to analyse the uncertainty involved.

The maximin basis

The maximin basis is short for 'maximising the minimum possible outcome'. This means that the decision maker will select the option that has the best outcome even if the worst situation arises. For example with the maximin rule option B would be selected from the following range of options.

	Option A Profit/(loss) $000	Option B Profit/(loss) $000	Option C Profit/(loss) $000
Best possible outcome	600	280	450
Worst possible outcome	(120)	80	(10)

Option B has the highest result if the worst possible outcome occurs. Thus a risk averse manager would select this option to avoid what might be disastrous consequences from the low outcomes for A and C, even though both these options offer the possibility of higher returns.

Perfect information

Perfect information is calculated by taking the difference between the EV of the best decision option (predicted on the basis of the perfect information) and the highest EV of profit if the perfect information is not available.

Risk neutral

The expected value is a weighted average, based on probabilities. Using probabilities means that the expected value outcome is based on what is likely as a long-term average and so no account is taken of whether the decision maker is risk averse or a risk seeker. Expected value decision rules assume that the decision maker is risk neutral, that is, prefers the most likely outcome.

Risk seeker

A risk seeker is a decision maker who is interested in the best outcomes no matter how small the chance that they may occur. They will choose the option which has the potential for the highest return.

Risk averse

A risk averse decision maker acts on the assumption that the worst outcome might occur. They will choose the option with the least amount of risk involved.

I hope that this helps.

Kind regards

Ola

Competency coverage

Sub-task	Technical		Business acumen		People		Leadership		M
1	Expected NPV and standard deviation	2.5							2
2	Choosing alternatives	2.5							2
3	Shadow price	6							
4	Limitations of expected value. Using maximin	3							
5	Risk neutral	6							
Total		20							2

CIMA P1 does not require competency in business acumen or leadership. People skills are only required for P1 in the form of decision making. The competency required for this question is therefore entirely technical, falling under the heading of core accounting and finance skills.

Task 12

Marking scheme

	Marks	Marks
Relevant cost statement for decision making		
Causes of overheads can be identified	2	
Statement shows the costs that can be avoided in different scenarios	2	
		4
Product discontinuation		
Advise product(s) to be discontinued	2	
Reasons for the above	2	
		4
How ABC can be used to improve decision making		
1-2 marks per valid point	Up to 12	
		12
MAXIMUM FOR TASK		20

Suggested solution

> From: Jatty Jones JJ@WTL.com
>
> To: Ketan Shah KS@WTL.com
>
> Sent: 25th August 20X5, 9.03 a.m.
>
> Subject: Relevant costs
>
> Dear Ketan,
>
> <u>Why the statement is suitable for decision making</u>
>
> When considering the financial implications of any decision, it is important to recognise the relevant costs that would be affected by a decision. Relevant costs are costs that will be incurred or saved as a direct result of the decision under consideration.
>
> Whilst showing costs and revenues for each product, the profit statement you produced makes and uses assumptions to attribute overheads to each product. There is no distinction between general overhead costs and product-specific overhead costs that would be avoided if the product were to be discontinued.
>
> The profit in my statement identifies the sales revenue, variable costs, contribution and directly attributable fixed costs for each product. This provides information that can assist with decision-making, both for our normal operational purposes and also to assist with decisions about the continuation or discontinuation of individual products.

Recommendation about discontinuation of products

The statement shows that all four products make a positive contribution towards fixed overhead costs and profit. It also shows the financial effect that discontinuing each of the products would have on profit. This is shown by the total contribution earned by each product minus the fixed overhead costs that are directly attributable to the product.

Our profits would fall if any of products X, Y or Z were discontinued, but profits would have been higher by $30,000 in the period if product W had not been made and sold.

By discontinuing production of product W, we may therefore be able to increase profits in future periods. Ending production of product W would mean that there will be spare machine hour capacity and it may be possible to increase profits further by using this capacity to increase output of the other products.

How activity based costing can be used in a retail environment

More realistic pricing

Activity based costing (ABC) helps to address one of the main problems with traditional costing systems – that is, excessive costs are often charged to high-volume products (product-cost subsidisation). This problem could lead to the low-volume products being under-priced, probably leading to increased customer demand (and vice versa for high volume products). As ABC is based on a fairer system – with costs being allocated using cost drivers that cause the costs to occur in the first place – it helps retail organisations to determine a more realistic price for individual products. This will reduce the likelihood of lower volume products being sold at unprofitable prices, and retailers being accused of predatory pricing.

Allocation of floor space to higher demand products

Linked with the more realistic pricing aspect of ABC, retailers will be able to more accurately predict demand when 'proper' prices are set. When demand can be more accurately predicted, it will be easier to allocate floor space according to this demand, which should help to improve profitability.

Diversity of products, processes and customers

Modern retail organisations deal with numerous products and sell a wide range of products. ABC assists in identifying activities required to support each category of product, for example, and the cost drivers of these activities. By doing so, ABC can help retail organisations to determine the 'real' cost of each category of product which will again help in the pricing process.

Demands on overhead resources

Different customers place different demands on overhead resources. In a retail environment where customers could be trade customers or members of the public, a member of the public is more likely to place more demands on available resources (such as the advice centre) than a trade customer who has used our products many times before. By allocating overheads according to cost drivers, we could distinguish prices between business customers and members of the public.

Kind regards

Jatty

Competency coverage

Sub-task	Technical		Business acumen		People		Leadership		Max
1	Relevant cost statement for decision making	4							4
2	Product discontinuation	4							4
3	Using ABC for decision making	12							12
Total		20							20

This task focuses directly on relevant costing and activity-based costing, both of which are core technical areas for P1.

Topic 5 – F1 Task Practice

Topic 5 – F1 Primary Tasks

Task 13 - JN Co

(indicative timings : 1st email 20 mins, 2nd email 10 mins, 3rd email 15mins)

Your name is Shelley Pees and you have recently been employed as a management accountant at JN Co. JN is a newly established company which produces children's films for the DVD and Blu-ray market. JN is owned and managed by James Nathan, a young entrepreneur who has a good understanding of his target market and a flair for creating new products.

James recently established the company when he inherited a cash sum of $250,000 from his grandfather, Donald. Donald also left him a contract for the production rights to a series of short films which tell the adventures of a group of woodland animals. James believes these films can become a best seller in the DVD and Blu-ray market and has estimated the future value of these to be $100,000.

Today is 2nd March 20X4.

It is your second day working for JN and James has asked you in to his office so that he can explain his future strategy for the business. He is very excited as he tells you about all of the investments he has already made as well as future plans that he has in order to strengthen the business in the coming years.

He tells you the following information:

- In order to promote his business James employed an external consultant to design JN's corporate logo and to create advertising material to promote JN's corporate image. The total cost of consultancy was $80,000.

- James recently spent $30,000 sending his production staff on a specialist training course. This was a relatively expensive course but James believes that this has led to a marked improvement in production quality and his staff now need less supervision. This has in turn led to an increase in revenue and cost reductions. The organiser of the course has stated that benefits from the training should last for a minimum of 3 years.

- James also tells you that he plans to spend $120,000 on a television advertising campaign. The campaign will be launched two months before the year end and will run for a 6 month period. James believes that increased sales as a result of the publicity will continue for two years from the start of the advertisements.

James is particularly pleased at how strong his financial statements will appear after all this investment and has asked you to prepare an email which summarises the accounting treatment of the production rights, consultancy, training and television advertising costs.

Write your email to James

A few days later James tells you that he is starting to realise that promoting his business has been very expensive and that he has spent a large proportion of the initial funds he invested in JN. James is aware that he will need to find a long-term solution to fund his business but for the moment he has arranged an overdraft facility with his bank. He is also aware that he could use a term loan to obtain short-term funding and has asked you to send him an email which discusses these two sources of short-term funding and which also includes details of any other short-term sources of finance that you think he should consider.

Write your email to James

Your first month working at JN has gone really quickly and the end of March is now approaching. Since he started trading James has not really been very aware of the tax implications of running a business! He has a meeting next week with a tax expert from an external firm of accountants who is going to talk him through the concept of and rules relating to corporate income tax. However he knows that corporate income tax is just one aspect of his tax responsibilities.

He has sent you the following email asking you for information.

From: James Nathan JN@JNCo.co.uk

To: Shelley Pees SP@JNCo.co.uk

Sent: 30th March 20X4, 08.22

Subject: Tax aspects of running a business

Dear Shelley,

Many thanks for all you have done so far! I hope you have enjoyed your first month with us? As you know I have a meeting with a tax expert next week to discuss corporate income tax. However I am a bit worried that I haven't fulfilled my tax responsibilities properly since I started trading so I need you to do three things for me please. Can you prepare a schedule for me which covers:

- The powers that the tax authorities have which may be relevant to me

- The records I need to keep to support my VAT returns

- The effect on my VAT calculations if we start to sell books as well as films. The films we sell are subject to VAT at the standard rate of 15%; however I am informed that books are zero rated. What does this mean?

Kind regards,

James

James Nathan

Managing Director

JN Co

E: JN@JNCo.co.uk

T: 0435 123765

Write your response to the email from James

Task 14 - KM

(indicative timings: 1st email 20 mins, 2nd email 7 mins)

Your name is Amelie Walters and you work as an assistant to the management accountant, Mable Peters, at KM. KM is resident in Country X and a retailer which sells small electrical appliances. KM has a year-end of 30th June 20X8.

Today is 12th July 20X8.

You are in the process of preparing the financial statements of KM for the year ended 30th June 20X8. Last week you printed off the trial balance generated by the accounting system and processed several journal entries relating to year-end adjustments (including depreciation and closing inventory). You gave this information to Mable Peters for review.

Having reviewed this information Mable has sent you the following email:

From: Mable Peters MP@KM.co.uk

To: Amelie Walters AW@KM.co.uk

Sent: 12th July 20X8, 10.27

Subject: KM Financial Statements for the year ended 30th June 20X8

Dear Amelie,

Many thanks for the work you have done on the financial statements so far. I have reviewed the information you have given me and it looks good. There are however, a few additional adjustments which need to be processed which I detail below:

(1)   An inventory count at the year-end valued inventory at $183,000. This value includes inventory that original cost $15,000 but is now obsolete and its estimated scrap value is $2,000.

(2)   On 1st June 20X8 KM issued 250,000 $1 equity shares at a premium of $75,000. Proceeds of $325,000 were received before 30th June 20X8 but the transaction has not been included in the trial balance.

(3)   On 7th July we were advised that one of our customers, PRW, is in financial difficulty and has gone into liquidation. It is unlikely that any of the $17,000 balance outstanding at 30th June 20X8 will be paid.

(4)   The sales revenue for the year to 30th June 20X8 includes $15,000 received from a new overseas customer. The $15,000 was a 10% deposit for an order of $150,000 worth of goods. KM is still waiting for the result of the new customer's credit reference and at 30th June 20X8 had not despatched any goods.

(5)   The patent acquired by KM on 1 July 20X2 cost $180,000 and was estimated to have a useful life of 10 years with no residual value. Amortisation for the year of $18,000 is still to be charged and this will leave the patent with a carrying value of $72,000 at 30th June 20X8. Finally the fair value of the patent at 30th June 20X8 was $65,000.

Can you please have a think about each of the above items and send me an email which explains your proposed accounting treatment and any adjustments required.

Kind regards,

Mable

Mable Peters, Management Accountant, KM

E: MP@KM.co.uk

T: 0145 593684

Write your email to Mable

It is now 23rd August and KM's financial statements are almost finalised. You have prepared KM's tax computation for Mable based on the tax rules that relate to KM. The tax rules are contained in Exhibit 1 and the tax computation you have prepared is shown in Exhibit 2.

Mabel has asked you to send her an email explaining the tax computation.

Exhibit 1:

Country X – Tax regime

Relevant tax rules

Corporate Profits

Unless otherwise specified, only the following rules for taxation of corporate profits will be relevant, other taxes can be ignored:

(a) Accounting rules on recognition and measurement are followed for tax purposes.

(b) All expenses other than depreciation, amortisation, entertaining, taxes paid to other public bodies and donations to political parties are tax deductible.

(c) Tax depreciation is deductible as follows:

- 50% of additions to property, plant and equipment in the accounting period in which they are recorded

- 25% per year of the written-down value (ie cost minus previous allowances) in subsequent accounting periods except that in which the asset is disposed of

- No tax depreciation is allowed on land

(d) The corporate tax on profits is at a rate of 25%.

(e) No indexation is allowable on the sale of land.

(f) Tax losses can be carried forward to offset against future taxable profits from the same business.

Value Added Tax

Country X has a VAT system which allows entities to reclaim input tax paid. In Country X the VAT rates are:

Zero rated   0%
Standard rated   15%

Exhibit 2:

KM tax computation

	$	$
Accounting profit per financial statements		190,000
Add back items of expense that are not tax allowable:		
Entertaining	9,800	
Amortisation	25,000	
Depreciation – property, plant and equipment	42,000	
Depreciation – vehicles ($18,000 ÷ 6 years)	3,000	
		79,800
		269,800
Deduct items of income that are not taxable or tax allowances given:		
Tax depreciation – property, plant and equipment	65,000	
Tax depreciation – vehicles ($18,000 × 50%)	9,000	
		(74,000)
Taxable profit		195,800
Tax due		$48,950

Write your email to Mabel

Task 15 - Delta Co

(indicative timings : 1st email 12 mins, 2nd email 12 mins, 3rd email 12mins)

Your name is Lucy Heffley and you work as a management accountant at Delta Co. Delta is a large company that manufactures and sells motor vehicles. It has a year-end of 31 December 20X1.

Delta's Board of Directors have recently been reviewing the company's extensive property portfolio. Over the years it has invested heavily in the acquisition of property. Some properties are used in Delta's manufacturing activities; others are used as show rooms from which the motor vehicles are sold and others are used for administrative purposes.

Delta would like to be in a position to invest in the production of a new brand of motor vehicle in the next two years but needs cash resources to do this. One proposal that the Board is currently considering is to streamline their property portfolio in order to generate the required cash.

Today is 7th April 20X1.

You have received the following email from Laila Wheeler, Finance Director at Delta Co:

From: Laila Wheeler LW@Delta.co.uk

To: Lucy Heffley LH@Delta.co.uk

Sent: 7th April 20X1, 09.15

Subject: Delta Co's property portfolio

Dear Lucy,

You will be aware that the Board is currently working on several proposals to streamline Delta's property portfolio with the aim of generating the cash needed for the production of a new brand of motor vehicle.

At the moment properties don't seem to be realising their full value in the sales market and so the Board is considering renting out one of Delta's surplus properties.

Delta has a building which is currently used for administration purposes which we no longer need. We bought the building some years ago for a cost of $600,000 and it has a current carrying amount of $486,000. The current fair value of the building is $800,000 and we have a prospective tenant who is interested in renting it from us. We would expect the fair value of the building to increase to $825,000 by the end of the year.

The Board plans to treat this building as an investment property under IAS 40 *Investment Properties* using the fair value model.

Please can you advise me as to whether this is appropriate and also consider the impact that this decision would have on Delta's cash flow and its financial statements.

Kind regards,

Laila

Laila Wheeler, Finance Director, Delta

E: LW@Delta.co.uk

Write your email to Laila

It is now 27th April and the new tenant is in the building.

Plans to produce the new brand of motor vehicle are still on-going but the Board now feels that they will need a new production facility to produce the vehicles because the technology required is not available in their current manufacturing facilities. The plan is to acquire the new production facility, and then once the new facility is fully operational, sell off one of the existing manufacturing plants. However, there will undoubtedly be a time delay between paying for the new production facility and selling off the existing one. As such Delta will need to use some of its existing loan facility or take out a long-term loan to finance the project and the Board is concerned about the impact that the finance charges will have on Delta's profit.

Laila Wheeler has sent you the following email:

From: Laila Wheeler LW@Delta.co.uk

To: Lucy Heffley LH@Delta.co.uk

Sent: 27th April 20X1, 13.52

Subject: New production facility

Dear Lucy,

The Board is now turning their attention to providing Delta with the new production facility that it needs in order to produce the new brand of motor vehicle. This facility will be a high-tech facility and as such will need to be purpose-built.

At the present time the Board is intending that Delta will build the new production facility itself and is aware that under IAS 23 *Borrowing Costs* certain costs need to be capitalised.

Please would you drop me an email which explains the circumstances when, and the amount at which, borrowing costs should be capitalised so that I can share this information with the Board.

Kind regards,

Laila

Laila Wheeler, Finance Director, Delta

E: LW@Delta.co.uk

T: 0173 496285

Write your email to Laila

The end of June is now approaching and Laila Wheeler is briefing you about the management accounts that will need to be produced for the first six months of the year. Laila has told you that the Board are concerned that Delta has taken out several long-term loans during the first half of the year and that this will have a negative impact on its financial statements. Consequently Laila has asked you to produce two sets of financial information relating to Delta's properties based on information she has given you.

You have done this and these are shown in Exhibit 1. These figures do not include the investment property or the new production facility but do show Delta's five other properties. The figures in column A have been prepared using the same accounting policies as in the prior year financial statements whereas the figures in column B include Delta's head office (property 4) at a revalued

BPP
LEARNING MEDIA

amount. The reason for this is that it is located in the centre of London where property prices have risen substantially over recent years. All properties were previously held at historic cost and have a 50 year life.

Exhibit 1:

Delta's property (excluding the investment property and the new production facility)		
	Column A $'000	Column B $'000
Cost/ valuation		
Property 1 (held for 20 years)	700	700
Property 2 (held for 15 years)	400	400
Property 3 (held for 12 years)	650	650
Property 4 (held for 13 years)	550	900
Property 5 (held for 4 years)	200	200
	2,500	2,850

	Column A $'000	Column B $'000
Accumulated depreciation		
Property 1	280	280
Property 2	120	120
Property 3	156	156
Property 4	143	0
Property 5	16	16
	715	572
Carrying amount	1,785	2,278
Revaluation surplus	0	493

Having had a few days to consider the figures you have prepared for Laila you are starting to feel uneasy about the prospect of Laila showing these figures to the Board.

Prepare an email to Laila which will accompany the figures in Exhibit 1. You should explain any concerns you have regarding the proper application of accounting standards and any ethical concerns you have.

Write your email to Laila

Task 16 - AD Co
(indicative timings : 1st email 18 mins, 2nd email 9 mins)

Your name is Sandy Lee and you work as a management accountant at AD Co. AD operates five factories in different locations in Country X. Each factory manufactures a different product line and each product line is treated as a separate segment under IFRS 8 Operating Segments.

One factory which produces a range of shoes, forecast an increased annual loss of $2,000,000 for the year to 31 March 20X9. On 1 March 20X9 AD's management decided to close the factory and cease the sale of its range of shoes. Closure costs, net of any gains on disposal of the assets, are estimated to be $150,000.

Today is 4th April 20X9.

You have received the following email from AD's finance director, Barney Ross:

From: Barney Ross BR@AD.co.uk

To: Sandy Lee SL@AD.co.uk

Sent: 4th April 20X9, 09.25

Subject: Closure of shoe factory

Dear Sandy,

As you know the Board are in the process of closing our shoe factory and I wanted to give you an update on the information I have so far and also the considerations we need to make for the year-end financial statements.

As of 31st March 20X9 our management team are still negotiating payment terms with the shoe factory workforce and have not agreed an actual closure date. Therefore, the Board have not yet attempted to find a buyer for the factory or its assets.

The Board want to completely exclude the shoe factory results from AD's financial statements for the year-ended 31st March 20X9 as they feel that because the shoe factory is about to be closed or sold, including the results of the shoe factory in the results for the year would mislead investors.

Please can you prepare a briefing note that I can use to respond to the Board on this issue. You should consider the requirements of International Financial Reporting Standards and also any ethical issues.

Many thanks,

Barney

Barney Ross, Finance Director, AD

E: BR@AD.co.uk

T: 0172 592578

Write your email to Barney

It is now 22nd April 20X9 and the external auditors are arranging to begin their audit fieldwork and testing at AD's premises.

Barney Ross sends you a second email:

From: Barney Ross BR@AD.co.uk

To: Sandy Lee SL@AD.co.uk

Sent: 22nd April 20X9, 16.18

Subject: External audit

Dear Sandy,

Thank you for your briefing note on the required treatment of the shoe factory. The Board have accepted that the results of the shoe factory do need to be shown in AD's financial statements and they are planning to show the results of the shoe factory as a discontinued operation.

The external auditors will soon be with us and I'm sure this is something that they will examine in detail.

Could you please outline for me the likely response of the external auditors in relation to this issue? I'd also like to know the impact this issue will have on their audit report based on the financial statements as they currently stand.

Many thanks

Barney

Barney Ross, Finance Director, AD

E: BR@AD.co.uk

T: 0172 592578

Write your email to Barney

Task 17 - P Co

(indicative timings : 1st email 18 mins, 2nd email 16 mins)

Your name is Peony Hills and you are the management accountant at P Co a textile company which manufactures clothing for high street retailers. P Co has been trading successfully for 12 years but has recently found that there have been many changes in the market place which has meant that competition to obtain contracts is fierce and profit margins are falling.

The Board of Directors of P Co have held a series of meetings with senior management to try to overcome what they perceive to be one of the key threats to their business. They have decided that in order to be successful they need to reduce their inventory purchase and holding costs without compromising on the quality of their products.

Today is 7th February 20X2.

You receive the following email from Fred Jones, Finance Director of P Co.

From: Fred Jones FJ@PCo.co.uk

To: Peony Hills PH@PCo.co.uk

Sent: 7th February 20X2, 10.04

Subject: Inventory procurement

Dear Peony,

You will be aware the Board have been working on a series of strategies recently to try to ensure the continued success of P Co. One area which we have identified as requiring improvement is inventory procurement. In the past we have used many different methods to manage the inventory ordering and holding system but none have been particularly successful.

The Board would like you to perform some research into Just-in-Time systems ("JIT") and the Economic Order Quantity model ("EOQ"). We would particularly like you to:

- Explain the EOQ model and the JIT approach to inventory management and how they differ
- Explain any major requirements for the successful operation of a JIT system

I will be able to give you more details later, but another strategy the Board is considering is to acquire a controlling interest in a fabric/ materials manufacturer so please consider the impact this may have on your research.

Kind regards,

Fred

Fred Jones

Finance Director

P Co

E: FJ@PCo.co.uk

Write your email to Fred

It is now **5th October 20X2** and a lot has happened over the last 8 months. The Board of Directors considered your report on the EOQ model and a JIT system and decided that the best way forward was to acquire a controlling interest in a supplier and then implement a JIT system.

As a result P Co acquired 80% of S Co on 1 July 20X2 and you have just produced the first set of consolidated financial statements for the P Co group for the year ended 30 September 20X2.

An extract from the consolidated financial statements can be found in Exhibit 1.

Exhibit 1

Consolidated financial statements (extract) for the year ended 30 September 20X2			
	P Co	S Co	Consolidated
	$'000	$'000	$'000
Consolidated Statement of Financial Position			
Current assets			
Inventories	10	42	46
Due from P Co	-	117	0
Cash and cash equivalents	65	81	163
Current liabilities			
Due to S Co	100	0	0
Consolidated Statement of Profit or Loss			
Revenue	2,515	540	2,560
Cost of sales	(1,306)	(408)	(1,324)
Gross profit	1,209	132	1,236
Other expenses	(800)	(84)	(821)
Profit for the period	U 409	U 48	U 415

Notes:

(1)   P Co acquired 80% of S Co on 1 July 20X2.

(2)   Since 1 July 20X2 S Co made sales to P Co of $90,000. S Co operates using a mark-up of 25%. $33\frac{1}{3}$% of these items were held in inventory at the year-end leading to unrealised profit of $6,000.

(3)   S Co's profit is deemed to accrue evenly throughout the period.

(4)   There was cash in transit of $17,000 at the year end.

After looking at the extract from the consolidated financial statements, Fred sends you the following email.

From: Fred Jones FJ@PCo.co.uk

To: Peony Hills PH@PCo.co.uk

Sent: 5th October 20X2, 16.17

Subject: Consolidated financial statements for the year ended 30th September 20X2

Dear Peony,

Many thanks for completing the consolidated financial statements so quickly. I need to present this information to the Board of Directors next week and need you to prepare some notes to help me with this.

Can you please email me a commentary which explains each of the amounts in the extract and which particularly addresses why the consolidated financial statements do not simply show the two companies added together.

Kind regards,

Fred

Fred Jones

Finance Director

P Co

E: FJ@PCo.co.uk

T: 0135 975385

Write your email to Fred

Task 18 - AM Co

(indicative timing : 1st email 25 mins, 2nd email 13 mins)

Your name is Matthew Moore and you work as a management accountant at AM Co. AM provides specialist contract cleaning services to industrial customers and has seen an increase in its sales revenue in recent months. All sales are on credit.

More favourable credit terms are offered to larger customers (class A customers) which are required to pay within 60 days of invoicing. Smaller customers (class B customers) are required to pay within 30 days of invoicing. All sales are invoiced at the end of the month regardless as to when the sale is made.

On 2nd April 20X4 you returned from two weeks annual leave to find an email in your inbox from Freddie Jones, the Finance Director at AM. Freddie asked you to submit AM's cash flow forecast for the three months ending 31st July 20X4 based on the projected sales information he gave you.

You prepared the cash flow forecast on 3rd April 20X4 and sent it to Freddie Jones. The forecast is included in Exhibit 1.

Exhibit 1:

AM Co Cash flow forecast for the 3 months ending 31st July 20X4

	May $'000	June $'000	July $'000
Cash from receivables:	407	462	405
Cash paid:			
Payables	(284)	(256)	(271)
Other expenses	(129)	(114)	(123)
Final loan repayment		(50)	
Dividend	(20)		
Purchase of machinery items			(100)
Net cash flow	**(26)**	**42**	**(89)**
Cash balance b/fwd	15	(11)	31
Cash balance c/fwd	(11)	31	(58)

On receipt of your cash flow forecast Freddie sends you the following email:

From: Freddie Jones FJ@AM.co.uk

To: Matthew Moore MM@AM.co.uk

Sent: 4rd April 20X4, 15.41

Subject: AM Co's cash flow forecast for the 3 month's ending 31st July 20X4

Dear Matthew,

I hope you had a great holiday? Many thanks for the cash flow forecast that you prepared for me when you returned from annual leave.

I have reviewed it in detail and whilst everything seems to be correct the cash flow forecast itself is rather alarming. We seem to be benefitting from increased sales, especially to our class A customers and yet we find ourselves with a net cash outflow in two out of the three months you have covered. This doesn't make sense. Perhaps more worrying is that we only have a $50,000 overdraft facility with the bank and it appears that this will be breached.

Can you please have a think about what we can do to alleviate this cash flow position and send me an email which details:

(1)   How you suggest we get through the next 3 months without breaching our overdraft position; and:

(2)   The advantages and disadvantages of factoring as a method of managing our trade receivables

Kind regards,

Freddie

Freddie Jones, Finance Director, AM

E: FJ@AM.co.uk

T: 0158 390667

Write your email to Freddie

It is now 10th April and Freddie sends you the following email:

From: Freddie Jones FJ@AM.co.uk

To: Matthew Moore MM@AM.co.uk

Sent: 11th April 20X4, 12.34

Subject: Cash flow forecasts (again!)

Dear Matthew,

Thanks again for the information you gave me on how to improve our cash flow forecasts. We discussed this at yesterday's Board meeting and have decided to spread out the timing of the purchase of machinery items and talk to the bank about a short/ medium-term loan.

However, as we were discussing the cash flow forecasts one of the other directors asked whether we were confident in our sales forecasting as this obviously impacts our net cash flow forecasts. I am happy that our sales forecasting is a robust process but wondered if you could let me have a summary of why sales are often thought to be an organisation's principal budget factor and the factors to consider when preparing sales forecasts.

Many thanks,

Freddie

Freddie Jones, Finance Director, Delta

E: FJ@AM.co.uk

T: 0158 390667

Write your email to Freddie

Topic 5 – F1 Primary Tasks Solutions

Task 13

Marking scheme

	Marks	Marks

Email 1 – accounting treatment of "investments" made
Production rights:

	Marks	Marks
Conclusion - production rights cannot be an asset as recognition criteria not satisfied	1	
Discussion of recognition criteria:	1	
Asset	1	
Probable future economic benefit	1	
Reliable measurement		
Consultancy costs:		
Accounting treatment	1	
Reason for conclusion	1	
Training costs:		
Conclusion re prohibition from capitalisation	1	
Relevant accounting treatment	1	
Advertising costs:		
Accounting treatment as an expense in SPL	1	
Prepayment	1	
Reason for conclusion	1	
Maximum for email 1		11

Email 2 – sources of short term funding
Overdraft vs. term loan:

	Marks	Marks
Overdraft higher risk as repayable on demand	1	
Bank may be uncomfortable with a growing overdraft	1	
Overdraft has a variable rate – exposure to interest rate risk	1	
Term loans can be negotiated for a specific timescale/ scheduling repayment	1	
New company – term loan interest rate may be higher unless security is available	1	
Other sources:		
Delay payments to suppliers	1	
Improve credit control	1	
Available for email 2	7	
Maximum for email 2		5

Email 3 – tax queries
Powers of tax authorities:

	Marks	Marks
Power to examine records	½	
Power to request special reports, forms, returns	½	
Power to review and query filed returns	½	
Powers of entry and search	½	

BPP
LEARNING MEDIA

Application to JN Co:	1
Ability to review records since JN started trading	1
Ability to request specific information where information has not been provided	
Records:	
½ mark per record up to a maximum of 2 marks	2
VAT:	
Charging VAT on sales	1
Reclaiming VAT on purchases	1
Maximum for email 3	8
MAXIMUM FOR TASK	24

Suggested solution

Email 1

From: Shelley Pees SP@JNCo.co.uk

To: James Nathan JN@JNCo.co.uk

Sent: 3rd March 20X4, 11.27

Subject: Accounting treatment of "investments" made to date

Dear James,

Please find below a summary of the required accounting treatment of the production rights, consultancy, training and television advertising costs.

Production rights

Unfortunately the production rights cannot be recognised as an intangible asset in the financial statements because they do not satisfy the recognition criteria given in the IASB's Conceptual Framework for Financial Reporting.

In order to be recognised as an intangible asset, the recognition criteria would require the production rights to satisfy the definition of an asset, bring probable future economic benefit to JN and be capable of being measured reliably. There is little doubt that the production rights are an asset as JN has a contract giving control over the rights and it is also probable that they will bring future economic benefit to the business. However, the production rights were effectively a gift to the business from your grandfather and have no reliable monetary value. I realise that this is disappointing especially as you have estimated that the production rights will bring $100,000 of benefit to JN; however, this amount could not be externally verified at the date the rights were acquired.

Consultancy costs

Again it is not possible to recognise the consultancy costs as an intangible asset. Although the cost of the consultancy fees at $80,000 is known, it is virtually impossible to quantify any change in the value of the image of JN. Since the cost of the corporate image cannot be measured reliably, the

consultancy fees should not be recognised as an asset but should instead be classified as an expense in profit or loss in the year they are incurred.

Training costs

Although having well trained staff undoubtedly adds value to JN, the accounting standard IAS 38 *Intangible Assets* specifically prohibits the capitalisation of training costs. This is because JN has insufficient control over the expected future economic benefits arising from staff training. Trained staff are free to leave JN and find work with another company. Training is therefore part of the general cost of developing a business as a whole and so the $30,000 cost incurred must be shown as an expense in profit or loss.

Advertising costs

Expenditure on advertising is likely to bring future economic benefit to JN however the amount of the benefit is uncertain and beyond JN's control. As such the costs should be shown as an expense in profit or loss (and therefore not included as a current asset in the statement of financial position). However, given that the advertising campaign will run for two months of the current accounting period and for four months of the next year, a prepayment of $80,000 ($^4/_6 \times $120,000$) should be recognised within current assets at the year end.

Kind regards,

Shelley

Email 2

From: Shelley Pees SP@JNCo.co.uk

To: James Nathan JN@JNCo.co.uk

Sent: 10th March 20X4, 15.14

Subject: Short-term funding

Dear James,

Please find below some considerations regarding the use of a bank overdraft and a term loan as a source of short-term funding.

Overdraft vs. term loans

- An overdraft is generally repayable on demand and therefore carries a higher level of risk than a term loan where money is loaned for a specified term/ period.

- The bank may become uncomfortable with a growing overdraft and seek to secure scheduled repayment or other conditions from the company. Therefore, if JN continues to grow this may result in cash flow problems.

- Overdrafts are often subject to a floating/ variable interest rate which will expose JN to interest rate risk. A term loan can often be negotiated at a fixed rate which will give JN better certainty when forecasting cash flows.

- Term loans can be negotiated over a timescale that is better suited to JN's need for finance. For example, if you have a timescale in mind by which you will have secured long-term

financing then the repayment schedule can be tailored to JN's requirements, either using stage payments or by scheduling a single repayment once long-term funding is obtained.

- JN is a newly established company so it won't have a long trading record to secure a lower rate of interest on a term loan but it may have assets it could offer as security in order to reduce the interest rate.

Other sources of short-term finance

Sources most relevant to JN would include:

- Delay payments to suppliers although you must be careful not to lose supplier goodwill or damage JN's reputation
- Improve credit control procedures to accelerate cash collection from receivables

Please let me know should you need further information.

Kind regards

Shelley

Email 3

From: Shelley Pees SP@JNCo.co.uk

To: James Nathan JN@JNCo.co.uk

Sent: 30th March 20X4, 16.58

Subject: Tax queries

Dear James,

Thank you for your email and I have answered your queries below. Let me know if you need anything else.

Powers of tax authorities:

- Power to examine records
- Power to request special reports, forms or returns
- Power to review and query filed returns
- Powers of entry and search

When the tax authorities examine records they can go back several years. So if you have not provided them with the information they require it is possible that they will want to review your records since you started trading.

They generally only request special reports or query returns if it appears that full information has not been provided. Again, in your case if no information has been provided it is likely that the tax authorities will require specific information.

Powers of entry and search are only really likely to be used where fraud is suspected or the tax authorities have decided to conduct a VAT inspection.

Records to support VAT returns:

- Orders and delivery notes

- Purchase and sales invoices
- Credit and debit notes
- Purchase and sales books
- Cash books and receipts
- Bank statements
- VAT account

Effect on VAT of selling books (a zero rated product)

The good news here is that if you start to sell books, there will be very little change to your VAT requirements. At the moment you charge VAT at 15% on the films you sell and you reclaim the VAT suffered on the purchases you make.

If you sell zero rated books you will still charge VAT on these sales but at a rate of 0%. You will also be able to continue to reclaim all of your VAT suffered on purchases.

Kind regards

Shelley

Competency coverage

Sub-task	Technical		Business acumen		People		Leadership		Max
1	Production rights	3	Production rights	1					
	Consultancy	1	Consultancy	1					
	Training	1	Training	1					
	Advertising	2	Advertising	1					11
2	Short-term finance (maximum)	2	Short-term finance (maximum)	3					5
3	Powers	2	Powers	2					
	Records	2							
	VAT on sales	1	VAT on purchases	1					8
Total		14		10					24

The area of intangible non-current assets which is tested in email 1 is a technical area but this email requires students to decide on the correct accounting treatment (these are technical marks) and also explain why this is the case and these marks fall into business acumen. Short-term finance is a very familiar area and so a small proportion of marks have been awarded for the technical content but the business acumen marks are for where the student has considered the age and nature of JN Co's business and applied their knowledge. Powers of tax authorities, records and VAT are knowledge based areas and so marks are largely awarded for technical

understanding however business acumen marks are available where the student has thought again about the status of JN Co's business and applied this technical knowledge to the scenario.

Task 14

Marking scheme

	Marks	Marks
Email 1 – accounting treatment of adjustments		
Inventory:		
Correct accounting treatment	1	
Reason – lower of cost and NRV	1	
Share issue:		
Correct accounting treatment	1	
Disclosure in SOCIE	1	
Liquidation of PRW:		
Correct accounting treatment	1	
Reason – IAS 10 adjusting event	1	
Revenue deposit:		
Correct accounting treatment	1	
Reason	1	
Patent:		
Amortisation for the year	1	
Impairment	1	
Application to the business	<u>1</u>	
Maximum for email 1		11
Email 2 – corporate income tax		
PBT	½	
Entertaining	½	
Amortisation	½	
Depreciation – PPE	½	
Depreciation – vehicle	½	
Tax depreciation – PPE	½	
Tax depreciation – vehicle	1	
Maximum for email 2		<u>4</u>
MAXIMUM FOR TASK		<u>15</u>

Suggested solution

Email 1

From: Amelie Walters AW@KM.co.uk

To: Mable Peters MP@KM.co.uk

Sent: 13th July 20X8, 14.53

Subject: KM Financial Statements for the year ended 30th June 20X8

Dear Mabel,

Please find below a summary of the accounting treatment for each of the items detailed in your email and the required adjustments.

Inventory

At the end of the year inventory needs to be valued at the lower of cost and net realisable value. Currently the inventory is included in the financial statements at $183,000. However, this includes items which cost $15,000 and yet have a net realisable value of $2,000. Consequently, closing inventory should be reduced by $13,000 ($15,000 – $2,000). This will reduce both profit for the period (as cost of sales will increase) and current assets.

Share issue

The share issue needs to be recognised in the financial statements. KM received proceeds of $325,000 from the share issue. In the statement of financial position share capital should be increased by $250,000 and the share premium by $75,000. The $325,000 proceeds received should be added to cash and cash equivalents in current assets.

The movement in share capital and share premium also needs to be disclosed in the statement of changes in equity.

Liquidation of PRW

The notification that PRW has gone into liquidation would be classified as an adjusting event under IAS 10 *Events After the Reporting Period*. As such an adjustment should be to reduce receivables and profit for the period by $17,000. The expense is likely to be classified as an administrative expense in the statement of profit or loss.

Revenue deposit

The $15,000 recognised as revenue relates to a deposit for sales of goods that KM will despatch next year and so should not be included in revenue for the year ended 30th June 20X8. As such revenue (and profit for the period) should be reduced and the amount reclassified as "other payables" within current liabilities in the statement of financial position.

Patent

A full year's amortisation of $18,000 needs to be charged on the patent. This will be recognised as an expense in profit or loss and will reduce the patent's carrying value to $72,000. However the patent also appears to have suffered an impairment. At 30th June 20X8 the patent's carrying value will be $72,000 but it has a fair value of only $65,000. The patent is held at historic cost and so the impairment loss of $7,000 ($72,000 – $65,000) would be charged as an expense to profit or loss. This would effectively be recognised as additional amortisation which in turn reduces the carrying value of the patent to $65,000 in the statement of financial position.

Please let me know should you require further information.

Kind regards

Amelie

Email 2

From: Amelie Walters AW@KM.co.uk

To: Mable Peters MP@KM.co.uk

Sent: 24th August 20X8, 12.17

Subject: KM Tax Computation

Dear Mabel,

As requested I have prepare an explanation of KM's tax computation.

The tax computation starts with the accounting profit per the statement of profit or loss and this is then adjusted for items that are not accounted for and taxed in the same way and any tax allowances.

The entertaining expenses of $9,800 are added back as these have decreased the accounting profit before tax but are not an allowed expense for tax purposes according to the tax rules.

Amortisation and depreciation are also added back because these expenses have reduced the accounting profit before tax. Amortisation and depreciation are accounting adjustments calculated based on KM's accounting policies for non-current assets. Such policies are subjective and variable across different entities and so these expenses are added back to the accounting profit figure and instead universal tax allowances are given based on the tax rules.

Tax depreciation is given based on the tax rules. In the year that an asset is acquired, as in the case of the vehicles, an allowance amounting to 50% of the cost of the asset is awarded. Thereafter tax allowances are given at a rate of 25% based on the tax written down value of the asset (cost less accumulated tax allowances). Tax depreciation is awarded to compensate the KM for any wearing out in the asset's value. It reduces the taxable profit figure and ultimately to amount of tax KM would pay.

The actual amount of tax to be paid to the tax authorities is calculated by taking the taxable profit and multiplying this by the current tax rate of 25% (per the tax rules).

I hope this explains the tax computation however, please let me know should you require any further information.

Kind regards

Amelie

Competency coverage

Sub-task	Technical		Business acumen		People		Leadership		M
1	Inventory	1	Inventory	1					
	Share issue	2							
	Liquidation	1	Liquidation	1					
	Revenue	1	Revenue	1					
	Patent	2	Patent	1					
2	Corporate income tax (maximum)	4							
Total		11		4					

The adjustments to the financial statements will earn technical marks for the correct accounting treatments. Business acumen marks will be awarded for the explanation of the accounting treatment and its justification/ application from the accounting standard.

The explanation of the corporate income tax calculation is a technical exercise and so all marks are awarded for technical content.

Task 15

Marking scheme

	Marks	Marks
Email 1 – investment properties		
Can be an investment property if not used by Delta	1	
Calculation of revaluation gain pre classification	1	
Accounting treatment/ disclosure of revaluation gain	1	
Treatment of investment property under fair value model	1	
Treatment of any change in fair value	1	
Impact on cash flow	1	
Maximum for email 1		6
Email 2 – borrowing costs		
Qualifying asset	1	
Qualifying borrowing costs	1	
Accounting treatment of interest where borrowings are specific	1	
Accounting treatment of interest where borrowings are general	1	
Capitalisation period:		
Start	1	
Suspension	1	
Cessation	1	
Maximum for email 2		7
Email 3 – ethical issues		
Choice of accounting policy under IAS 16	1	
Possible to change of accounting policy:		
Permitted if it more fairly reflects the business' activities	1	
Not permitted if done to improve financial statements	1	
Revaluation would help the Board offset liabilities	1	
Need to revalue all assets in same class	1	
Positive impact on financial statements but on-going cost of valuations	1	
Higher depreciation charge	1	
Maximum for email 3		7
MAXIMUM FOR TASK		20

Task 3

Email 1

From: Lucy Heffley LH@Delta.co.uk

To: Laila Wheeler LW@Delta.co.uk

Sent: 7th April 20X1, 16.12

Subject: Delta Co's property portfolio

Dear Laila

The proposal you describe is to transfer a building which is currently recognised as property, plant and equipment under IAS 16 *Property, Plant and Equipment* to be an investment property using the fair value model under IAS 40 *Investment Properties*.

Provided that the building is not used at all by Delta then it is possible to treat the building as an investment property.

The building has a current carrying amount of $486,000. At the date that the building is classified as an investment property it would be revalued under IAS 16. The revaluation gain of $314,000 ($800,000 – $486,000) will be recorded in:

- other comprehensive income in the statement of profit or loss and other comprehensive income

- revaluation surplus in the statement of financial position

- movement and closing position shown in the statement of changes in equity.

After this the building would be included as an investment property and valued at $800,000. As you propose to adopt the fair value model the building would not be subject to further depreciation but measured at fair value in the financial statements each year, and therefore the property value increased or decreased as appropriate. Any change in fair value would be shown in profit or loss. Therefore **if** the building has a fair value of $825,000 at the year-end it would be shown as an investment property at that value and the increase in fair value of $25,000 would be credited to profit or loss.

In terms of cash flow there is no cash impact on Delta from the revaluation or the classification of the building as an investment property. As it stands the only cash flow from this decision will be the rental income from the tenant (you may choose to invoice on a monthly or quarterly basis).

Please let me know should you require further information.

Kind regards

Lucy

Email 2

From: Lucy Heffley LH@Delta.co.uk

To: Laila Wheeler LW@Delta.co.uk

Sent: 28th April 20X1, 10.25

Subject: New production facility

Dear Laila

Please find below information as to how borrowing costs should be recognised under IAS 23 *Borrowing Costs*.

Qualifying assets

A qualifying asset is an asset that necessarily takes a substantial period of time to get it ready for its intended use or sale. In Delta's case it would be 'intended use' as we plan to build and then use the production facility.

Qualifying borrowing costs

Qualifying borrowing costs are borrowing costs incurred in the construction of a qualifying asset. This includes interest and other related borrowings costs. Such costs must be capitalised as part of the overall cost of the new production facility.

Delta has two financing options available – either to use some of its existing financing facilities or to take out a new loan specifically to fund this project.

Where funds are borrowed specifically to finance the construction of a qualifying asset, the amount of borrowing costs eligible for capitalisation will be the borrowing costs incurred (at the effective rate of interest) less any investment income earned on the temporary investment of those borrowings.

Where funds are borrowed generally and the borrowings attributable to a particular asset cannot be readily identified, the amount of borrowing costs eligible for capitalisation should be estimated by applying a weighted average interest rate to the funds used in constructing the asset.

Capitalisation period

Capitalisation of the borrowing costs should commence once expenditure and construction on the new production facility commences and borrowing costs are incurred.

Capitalisation should be suspended if there is a period of time during which construction is suspended (for example if there are delay due to planning or design issues or due to bad weather).

Capitalisation of the borrowing costs should cease when substantially all activities necessary to prepare the asset for its intended use or sale (use in Delta's case) are complete.

I hope this clarifies the position, please let me know if you need further information.

Kind regards

Lucy.

Email 3

From: Lucy Heffley LH@Delta.co.uk

To: Laila Wheeler LW@Delta.co.uk

Sent: 30th June 20X1, 11.47

Subject: Property figures for the management accounts

Dear Laila

I am attaching the figures you asked me to produce for you regarding Delta's properties. These can be found in Exhibit 1.

Unfortunately I have some reservations about the accuracy and suitability of these figures and have explained these below.

IAS 16 *Property, Plant and Equipment*

IAS 16 states that property, plant and equipment (PPE) should initially be recorded at cost but then offers a choice of accounting policy. This means that PPE can be carried at historic cost less depreciation and any impairment losses or alternatively it can be held at current cost and revalued to fair value less depreciation and any impairment losses. Delta has always used the first approach.

Ethical concerns

It is possible to adopt the second approach but this should be because this accounting policy more fairly reflects the activities of a business. It is not acceptable simply to change an accounting policy in order to improve the financial statements. In Exhibit 1 you can see that the adjustment to revalue the head office (property 4) has led to an overall increase in PPE of $493,000 and this would certainly off-set some of the recent increase in long term liabilities due to the loans that Delta has taken out.

I would therefore ask you and the Board to consider whether this treatment is really appropriate.

Furthermore IAS 16 requires that if an entity revalues one property it must revalue all assets within that class (i.e. all other properties held by Delta).

This may be positive news for the Board especially if the value of the other properties has increased. However it should be noted that the valuations must be kept up to date so that the carrying amount of the assets is not materially different from their fair value and so there will be an on-going cost to assess the fair value of all properties.

Finally you should note that depreciation will be charged on the fair value of the asset and so the depreciation charge in the statement of profit or loss under this approach is likely to be higher than under the cost model. This will place pressure on the profit figure. Delta could elect to transfer the excess depreciation charge from the revaluation surplus to retained earnings and this would be shown in the statement of changes in equity.

Please would you let me know what you think about the concerns I have listed above.

Many thanks

Lucy

Competency coverage

Sub-task	Technical		Business acumen		People		Leadership		Max
1	Investment property	5	Investment property impact on cash flow	1					6
2	Borrowing costs	7							7
3	IAS 16 requirements Ethical considerations re changing an accounting policy	3	IAS 16 requirements Ethical considerations re changing an accounting policy	1 3					7
Total		15		5					20

The areas of investment properties, borrowing costs and property, plant and equipment in emails 1 to 3 are testing students' understanding of the correct accounting treatment and so are awarded technical marks.

The ethical issues raised in email 3 require students to exercise judgement and therefore gain business acumen marks.

Task 16

Marking scheme

	Marks	Marks
Email 1 – closure of shoe factory		
Exclusion of factory:		
Current proposal is contrary to IFRS and unethical	1	
Financial statements would be distorted	1	
Misleading/ prohibited treatment	1	
Appropriate treatment:		
IFRS 5 treatment	1	
Discontinued operation	1	
IFRS 5 criteria – disposed of or held for sale	1	
Held for sale criteria (½ mark for each of the four criteria)	2	
Per scenario not held for sale	1	
IFRS 8 disclosure	1	
Maximum for email 1		10
Email 2 – external audit		
Consideration of materiality	1	
Issue – non-compliance with IFRS 5	1	
Material misstatement – material but not pervasive	1	
Request that Board amend the financial statements	1	
Qualified – except for	1	
Maximum for email 2		5
MAXIMUM FOR TASK		15

Suggested solution

Email 1

From: Sandy Lee SL@AD.co.uk

To: Barney Ross BR@AD.co.uk

Sent: 4th April 20X9, 16.19

Subject: Closure of shoe factory

Dear Barney,

I am attaching a briefing note which addresses the required treatment of the shoe factory in the financial statements and the related ethical issues.

Please let me know should you require further information.

Kind regards

Sandy

Briefing note – closure of shoe factory

This briefing note address the financial reporting and ethical issues surrounding the proposed exclusion of the factory from AD's financial statements and also the required accounting treatment.

Exclusion of factory results

The Board's current proposal to completely exclude the results of the shoe factory from AD's financial statements is contrary to the requirements of International Financial Reporting Standards and is also unethical. This is because excluding the results of the shoe factory would distort the overall results of the company, making AD appear to be more profitable than it currently is. This would then mislead users of the financial statements and is prohibited.

If the results of the factory were to be completely excluded this would also breach two of the fundamental principles of the CIMA Code of Ethics for accountants. This Code requires professional accountant to demonstrate professional behaviour and comply with the relevant laws and standards when performing their duties. They should also act with integrity and this requires them to be honest in their work.

Appropriate treatment of the factory

The issue here is whether the factory can or should be classified as a discontinued operation according to IFRS 5 *Non-current Assets Held for Sale and Discontinued Operations*.

If this were the case then the loss made by the factory in the year should be separately disclosed in the statement of profit or loss and shown after profit from continuing operations. This disclosure would make it clear to users that the factory, although loss making, will not be part of AD's future operations.

However, IFRS 5 stipulates certain criteria which must be satisfied in order for the shoe factory to be classified as a discontinued operation. A discontinued operation is a component of an entity that has either been disposed of or is classified as held for sale under IFRS 5 and which represents a separate major line of business or geographical area of operations. The shoe factory is a separate major line of business; however it has not been disposed of at the year-end of 31st March 20X9 and so the question now remains as to whether the factory would be classified as held for sale.

To be classified as held for sale all of the following criteria must be satisfied:

(1) The factory must be available for immediate sale in its present condition; and

(2) The sale must be highly probable; and

(3) AD must be actively seeking a sale and committed to selling the factory; and

(4) The sale should be expected to be completed within one year of AD classifying the factory as held for sale.

The Board have not yet committed to a plan to find a buyer for the factory and so the sale is not highly probable. This means that the shoe factory cannot be classified as discontinued operation which is held for sale. As such, the financial statements must disclose the full loss made by the shoe factory within continuing operations in the statement of profit or loss (i.e. it should be disclosed in the same way as the other four factories.

Furthermore the external revenue; inter-segmental revenue; interest expense; interest revenue; segment profit; segment assets; segment liabilities and any expenditure by the segment on non-

BPP
LEARNING MEDIA

current assets would need to be disclosed in a note to the financial statements as required by IFRS 8 *Operating Segments.*

Kind regards,

Sandy

Email 2

From: Sandy Lee SL@AD.co.uk

To: Barney Ross BR@AD.co.uk

Sent: 23rd April 20X9, 10.53

Subject: External audit

Dear Barney,

AD has five factories each of which constitutes an operating segment according to IFRS 8 *Operating Segments.* Therefore it should be assumed that the results of the shoe factory are material to the financial statements as a whole. This means that the auditors will need to make sure that the shoe factory is accounted for and disclosed appropriately. This essentially means in accordance with IFRS 5.

At the current time the financial statements do not comply with the requirements of IFRS 5 as (per my earlier briefing note) the shoe factory cannot be disclosed as a discontinued operation.

The external auditors would therefore say that there is a material misstatement in the financial. The matter is likely to be material but not pervasive which means it is significant enough to affect users' understanding of the financial statements but not fundamental to their understanding.

It is likely that they will ask the Board to amend the financial statements and show the results of the shoe factory within continuing operations.

If the Board refuse to do this then the external auditors will modify their audit opinion and issue an audit report which summarises the incorrect treatment of the shoe factory. They will give a qualified audit opinion which means that except for this issue the financial statements present fairly AD's activities for the year ended 31st March 20X9.

The only way to avoid this modified audit opinion would be to amend the financial statements.

Kind regards,

Sandy

Competency coverage

Sub-task	Technical		Business acumen		People		Leadership		Max
1	IFRS 5 issues Ethical issues IFRS 8 issues	6 1	IFRS 5 issues Ethical issues IFRS 8 issues	3					10
2			External audit	5					5
Total		7		8					15

The knowledge tested in email 1 concerning IFRS 5 and IFRS 8 is purely technical content and these will be awarded technical marks.

However the ethical issues posed by the scenario and the implications for the external audit will earn business acumen marks as they test the regulation aspect of the syllabus.

Task 17

Marking scheme

	Marks	Marks
Email 1 – inventory procurement		
EOQ model:		
Purpose of the model	1	
Three assumptions	1	
JIT system:		
Purpose of the model	1	
Zero inventories/ perfect quality	1	
JIT purchasing	1	
JIT production	1	
Comparison:		
Demand	½	
Inventory holding	½	
Ordering costs vs. holding costs	½	
Wastage	½	
Requirements for a successful JIT operation:		
Timing of supplier deliveries	1	
Quality of supply	1	
Maximum for email 1		10
Email 2 – consolidated financial statements		
Consolidated statement of financial position		
Inventory:		
Inventory valuation principle	1	
Adjustment in consolidated financial statements	½	
Intra-group balances and cash and cash equivalents:		
Principles behind elimination	1	
Agreement of balances	1	
Adjustment in the consolidated financial statements	½	
Consolidated statement of profit or loss		
Principles:		
Show as one entity	½	
Consolidate from date control achieved	½	
Intra-group trading and unrealised profit:		
Remove intra-group trading	½	
Remove unrealised profit	1	
Adjustment in the consolidated financial statements - revenue	1	
Adjustment in the consolidated financial statements – cost of sales	1	
Other expenses	½	
Maximum for email 2		9
MAXIMUM FOR TASK		19

Suggested solution

Email 1

From: Peony Hills PH@PCo.co.uk

To: Fred Jones FJ@PCo.co.uk

Sent: 9th February 20X2, 15.19

Subject: Inventory procurement

Dear Fred,

Please find below an explanation of the EOQ model and the JIT approach to inventory management. I have also included some information on factors which would be critical to the success of a JIT system.

EOQ model

The EOQ model is a model which could suggest the most economic order size for P Co to place when replenishing inventory in order to minimise inventory ordering and holding costs.

The model is based on the following three assumptions although it should be noted that these may not be achievable for P Co:

(1)   Demand is constant and certain (i.e. no stock out costs);
(2)   Delivery is instantaneous or lead time is constant and;
(3)   Purchase costs are constant, i.e. no discounts exist for bulk purchasing

JIT system

JIT is a system whose objective is to produce or procure products or components as they are required by a customer for use, rather than to hold as inventory.

A JIT system would aim for P Co to hold zero inventories and have perfect quality. It is a pull system, which responds to demand, and for P Co would consist of JIT purchasing and JIT production.

JIT purchasing seeks to match the usage of materials with the delivery of materials from external suppliers so that materials inventories can be kept at near-zero levels.

JIT production is a system driven by demand for finished products. P Co would need to ensure that materials are only processed through a stage of production when they are needed by the next stage. This should result in minimal (or non-existent) inventory of work in progress and finished goods.

Comparison of the two systems

Demand:

The EOQ model is based on estimated demand whereas JIT is based on actual demand.

Inventory holding:

JIT is based on holding zero or very little inventory whilst the EOQ model is based on minimising inventory ordering and holding costs.

Ordering costs versus holding costs:

The EOQ model is based on estimated demand and will involve fewer inventory orders per year than JIT because each order level will be higher than a JIT order level. There are therefore lower ordering costs for EOQ which are matched by higher holding costs.

Wastage:

As JIT involves ordering inventory only as required it reduces the level of wastage.

Requirements for a successful JIT operation

JIT requires a very close relationship with suppliers which is illustrated in two main ways:

- Timing of supplier deliveries: P Co would need confidence that the supplier will deliver on time because there will be no buffer of inventory to fall back on and production would otherwise be delayed.

- Quality of supplier deliveries: P Co would need to be confident that the supplier would deliver materials of 100% quality so that there will be no rejects, returns or consequent production delays.

Please let me know should you require further information.

Kind regards

Peony

Email 2

From: Peony Hills PH@PCo.co.uk

To: Fred Jones FJ@PCo.co.uk

Sent: 7th October 20X2, 10.54

Subject: Consolidated financial statements

Dear Fred,

Please find below a commentary on the consolidated financial statements of the P Co group for the year ended 30th September 20X2.

Consolidated statement of financial position

Inventory:

The consolidated inventory figure must show inventory at the lower of cost and net realisable value to the group. During the year S Co has supplied goods at a sales value of $90,000 to P Co and at the year-end $33\frac{1}{3}$ % of these inventories are still held by P Co. This means that the inventory figure includes profit of $6,000 which is unrealised from a group perspective and so the inventory figure is too high because of the unrealised profit.

Therefore when calculating the consolidated inventory figure we aggregate the figures for P Co and S Co but remove the unrealised profit of $6,000.

Intra-group balances and cash and cash equivalents:

Intra-group balances are not shown in the consolidated financial statements because the aim of such statements is to present the financial statements as if the two companies were one single entity. Therefore the intra-group balances must be cancelled but they must first balance before this can be done. The balances did not agree due to the cash in transit at the year-end from P Co to S Co; this needs to be "pushed forward" to its final destination thereby reducing the receivable held by S Co and increasing cash and cash equivalents.

This is why the intra-group balances are shown as zero and the cash and cash equivalents figure are the amounts in P Co and S Co's individual financial statements plus the cash in transit.

Consolidated statement of profit or loss

Main principles:

When preparing the consolidated statement of profit or loss we again need to show the two companies as one single entity. S Co was acquired on 1 July 20X2, namely 3 months before the year end. As such we only obtained control on that date and therefore we will consolidate 100% of S Co's revenue, cost of sales and other expenses but only from 1 July 20X2.

Profits are deemed to accrue evenly so we will consolidate $3/12$ of S Co's revenue, costs of sales and other expenses for the period.

Intra-group trading and unrealised profit:

A group cannot trade with itself and so intra-group trading needs to be eliminated. Since acquisition S Co made sales of $90,000 to P Co and this intra-group trading is eliminated by reducing both group revenue and group cost of sales by $90,000.

Furthermore the effect of the unrealised profit on inventory needs to be reflected in the consolidated statement of profit or loss. The inventory figure is too high from a group perspective as discussed above and so we reduce closing inventory which in turn increases cost of sales.

The revenue figure therefore represents P Co's revenue plus $3/12$ of S Co's revenue less the intra-group trading of $90,000.

The cost of sales figure is P Co's cost of sales plus $3/12$ of S Co's cost of sales less the intra-group trading of $90,000 plus the unrealised profit of $6,000.

The other expenses relate to P Co's other expenses plus $3/12$ of S Co's other expenses.

Please let me know should you require further information.

Kind regards,

Peony

Competency coverage

Sub-task	Technical		Business acumen		People		Leadership		M
1	EOQ/ JIT	8	EOQ/ JIT	2					1
2	Consolidated financial statements	9							
Total		17		2					1

Email 1 requires both the technical explanation of the EOQ and JIT models but it also requires application of this information to P Co's business. Business acumen marks have be awarded to reflect the need to apply this technical information to P Co's business.

The explanation of adjustments to the consolidated financial statements is a technical area and so full marks are allocated to technical content.

Task 18

Marking scheme

	Marks	Marks
Email 1 – cash flow forecast		
Cash from receivables:		
Invoice more promptly	1	
Change sales mix to sell more to class B customers	1	
Cash paid:		
Payables - negotiate improved credit terms	1	
Final loan repayment – timing	1	
Dividend – amount and timing	1	
Purchase of machinery items – delay/ stagger	1	
Purchase of machinery items – lease option	1	
Overdraft facility:		
Increase facility/ use term loan	1	
Factoring:		
Advantages (1 mark per valid point – maximum 3 marks)	3	
Disadvantages (1 mark per valid point – maximum 3 marks)	<u>3</u>	
Maximum for email 1		14
Email 2 – principal budget factor		
Principal budget factor:		
Definition	1	
Examples (sales/ machine capacity)	1	
Importance of the principal budget factor	1	
Sales forecasting:		
Use of internal estimates (1 mark per explained point/ ½ mark if items are just listed – maximum 2 marks)	2	
Statistical techniques (1 mark per explained point/ ½ mark if items are just listed – maximum 2 marks)	<u>2</u>	
Maximum for email 2		<u>7</u>
MAXIMUM FOR TASK		<u>21</u>

151

Suggested solution

Email 1

From: Matthew Moore MM@AM.co.uk

To: Freddie Jones FJ@AM.co.uk

Sent: 6th April 20X4, 10.08

Subject: AM Co's cash flow forecast for the 3 month's ending 31st July 20X4

Dear Freddie

Cash flow forecasts

I have reviewed the cash flow forecasts and have the following suggestions as to how AM's cash flow could be improved.

Cash from receivables

Other than factoring our trade receivables (which is covered below) there are two main ways in which we could improve the cash received from customers.

Firstly we could invoice as soon as the service is provided rather than invoicing at the end of the month as is our current practice. This could mean that we reduce our credit period significantly. For example as our procedures currently stand we could carry out cleaning work on the 1st of the month but this would not be invoiced until the end of the month and our customers would then have an additional 30 or 60 days credit from the date of invoicing. If we were to invoice more regularly we would collect monies earlier and this may be sufficient to prevent us breaching our overdraft limit in July.

Secondly we could try to make a higher percentage of our sales to our class B customers and therefore receive payment in 30 days rather than 60 days. It is unlikely that we would be able to reduce the credit terms we offer to our class A customers but we could also standardise our credit terms and offer 30 day credit terms only to all new customer accounts. This again would help us to collect monies earlier and we may then be able to avoid breaching the overdraft limit.

Cash paid

Payables:

We could attempt to negotiate improved credit terms with our existing suppliers. In particular, suppliers currently offering us a 30 day credit period may agree to extend it to 60 days. In the event that we cannot re-negotiate credit terms we must ensure that we take full advantage of the credit period available to us but must also be careful not to lose supplier goodwill.

Final loan repayment:

It may be possible to have a meeting with the bank and attempt to make a smaller loan repayment in June and further payments in July and August. Alternatively AM could consider taking out a small short-term loan (such as a term loan) for some or all of the loan repayment amount in order to reduce the burden on AM's cash flow in June.

Dividend:

It may be possible to reduce the amount of the dividend or once again spread the timing over which the dividend is paid. For example a dividend of $10,000 could be paid in May and a further $10,000 in August. Alternatively it may be possible to make a bonus issue of shares instead of paying a cash dividend.

Purchase of machinery items:

This is probably the entry in the cash flow forecast which contributes most to AM's cash outflows. The purchase of the machinery could be delayed or staggered so that some items are purchased in July whilst others are purchased in August and September.

Another option is for AM lease or rent the machinery items rather than buy them outright. This would again spread the timing of the payments. It is also possible to buy some items and lease others.

Overdraft facility

One final option is to apply for a temporary increase in the overdraft facility or to take out a short/ medium-term loan to pay off part of the overdraft facility. It should be noted that the purchase of machinery items should ideally be made with medium to long term financing to reflect the nature of the asset.

Use of factoring as method to manage trade receivables

You also asked me to consider the possibility of using factoring to manage trade receivables. There are certainly advantages and disadvantages to this and these are detailed below:

Advantages:

There are both financial and non-financial advantages:

(1)   A factoring organisation would advance cash to AM against the security of the AM's receivables. AM would assign its receivables to the factor and then typically ask for an advance of funds against the debts. This is usually up to 80% of the value of the debts. This would give AM immediate cash in place of trade receivables asset.

(2)   AM could then pay its suppliers promptly and take advantage of any early payment discounts.

(3)   Growth can be financed through sales rather than by injecting fresh external capital.

(4)   AM would not incur the costs of running its own receivables ledger department.

(5)   If the factoring is 'without recourse' then the factor carries the risk of irrecoverable debts.

(6)   AM's managers do not have to spend their time on the problems of slow paying receivables.

(7)   AM could make use of the receivables management expertise that the factor has. For example, the factor may be able to perform better credit checks than is possible under AM's existing facilities.

Disadvantages:

Again there are both financial and non-financial disadvantages:

(1)   Customer perception: customers will be making payments direct to the factor which is likely to present a negative picture of the firm.

(2)   Reputation: factoring may indicate that the firm is in need of rapid cash, raising questions about its financial stability.

(3)   Factoring agencies may be expensive and it is possible that the benefits will not outweigh the costs.

(4)   Once a factoring arrangement is in place, it may be difficult to go back to having an in-house receivables ledger facility.

(5)   Working practices: the factor may attempt to influence the way that the company does business. For example, they may wish to 'vet' any potential new customers.

I hope this information is useful and will help you make a decision as to the way forward. Please let me know if I can be of any other assistance.

Kind regards

Matthew

Email 2

From: Matthew Moore MM@AM.co.uk

To: Freddie Jones FJ@AM.co.uk

Sent: 12th April 20X4, 10.08

Subject: Re: Cash flow forecast (again!)

Dear Freddie

Please find some information on principal budget factors and methods of sales forecasting.

What is the principal budget factor?

Known as the key budget factor or limiting budget factor, this is the factor which, at any given time, effectively limits the activities of an organisation. The principal budget factor is usually sales demand: a company is often restricted from making and selling more of its products because there would be no sales demand for the increased output at a price which would be acceptable/ profitable for the company.

The principal budget factor may also be machine capacity, distribution and selling resources, the availability of key raw materials or the availability of cash.

The principal budget factor is important because once this factor is identified then the rest of the budget can be prepared. For example, if sales are the principal budget factor then the production budget can only be prepared after the sales budget is complete.

Sales forecasting

There are two basic approaches to sales forecasting.

(i)   Use of internal estimates

In-house sales staff can forecast future sales using their experience and knowledge of the company and by considering the following factors.

(1)   Past sales patterns
(2)   Economic environment
(3)   Results of market research
(4)   Anticipated advertising

Competency coverage

Sub-task	Technical		Business acumen		People		Leadership		Max
1	Cash flow forecasts Factoring	6	Cash flow forecasts Factoring	8					14
2	Principal budget factors Sales forecasting	3 4							7
Total		13		8					21

The cash flow forecast has already been prepared and so the marks available are for its interpretation and making practical recommendations. As such these marks are given as business acumen marks.

The advantages and disadvantages of factoring are a knowledge based areas and so are awarded technical marks.

Considerations of principal budget factors and sales forecasting are also knowledge areas and so are awarded technical marks.

Topic 5 – F1 Further Tasks

Task 19 - JKL

(indicative timing : 45 mins)

JKL operates two pension plans for its employees; a defined benefit pension plan for members of senior management and a defined contribution pension plan for all other employees.

In the defined benefit pension plan, the fair value of the plan assets at 30 September 20X5 was $13.1 million. The present value of the plan obligations at 30 September 20X5 was $13.9 million. JKL currently adopts the IAS 19 *Employee benefits* (as revised in 2011) approach for the treatment of re-measurement gains and losses.

JKL operates in a country that uses a Pay-As-You-Earn (PAYE) system for collecting taxes from employees. Each employer is provided with information about each employee's tax position and tables showing the amount of tax to deduct each period. Employers are required to deduct tax from employees and pay it to the revenue authorities on a monthly basis

You are Jem Owen, a trainee management accountant at JKL. You receive the following email from your line manager.

From: Harry Broad, Head of Management Accounting
To: Jem Owen, Management Accountant
Sent: 10 October 20X5
Subject: Pensions and taxation

Dear Jem,

I am currently putting together some notes for a presentation on pensions and personal tax issues, and I would be grateful if you could provide me with some comments on the following points:

(1) As you know, JKL operates both a defined benefit and a defined contribution pension plan. Explain how each of these pension plans above will be accounted for in both the statement of profit or loss and other comprehensive income and the statement of financial position of JKL.

(2) For the defined benefit plan, explain the required treatment for remeasurement gains and losses in accordance with IAS 19 Employee benefits.

(3) From the perspective of the government, list three advantages of the PAYE system.

(4) Describe where employee tax is recorded in a set of financial statements.

(5) Explain the difference between tax evasion and tax avoidance, using the examples below to illustrate your answer.

Cee has reduced her tax bill by taking advice from a tax expert and investing her surplus cash in government securities. The income from government securities is free of tax.
Gee works as a night security guard for a local entity and also has a job working in a supermarket during the day. Gee has reduced his tax bill by declaring only his day job income on his annual tax return.
You should respond via email, addressing each point in turn.
Harry

Write your response to the email from Harry

Task 20 - Paladin plc

(indicative timing : 45 mins)

You are Clemy Houghton, a financial controller at Paladin plc, a group with several subsidiaries.

Paladin has owned 25% of Augusta for many years. At the 30 September 20X1 year end the other equity shares (75%) in Augusta were owned by many separate investors. Shortly after this date Spekulate (a company unrelated to Paladin) accumulated a 65% interest in Augusta by buying shares from the other shareholders. In May 20X2 a meeting of the board of directors of Augusta was held at which Paladin lost its seat on Augusta's board.

Paladin also has a subsidiary, Fraston, which has a branch office in France which provides services to customers and sells products. Fraston's head office is in Germany, where the production facility and head office are located. France and Germany have double tax treaties with each other based on the OECD Model Tax Convention.

Today is 31 August 20X2. You receive an email from Javier Lupo, the Finance Director of Paladin:

From: Javier Lupo
To: Clemy Houghton
Subject: Group structure

Dear Clemy

As you know our group structure is quite complicated and the new Managing Director would like me to explain to him the impact of our group relationships on the consolidated financial statements. To help me do this, could you put together some notes on the following issues:

(1)   Define what is meant by control and explain how this is determined according to IFRS 10 Consolidated financial statements. Can you also explain how this differs from significant influence?

(2)   An explanation of the accounting treatment of Augusta in the financial statements for the year ending 30 September 20X2.

(3)   Can you also make some notes on the tax implications of groups, specifically:

(a)   What is withholding tax and why do tax authorities use it?

(b)   Why do countries need to enter into double taxation agreements? What are the main methods giving double taxation relief?

(c)   In which country/countries Fraston will be regarded as resident for tax purposes and how the profits Fraston makes in France will be taxed.

Thanks Clemy, I appreciate your help,

Javier

Write your response to the email from Javier

Task 21 - Accountancy Training

(indicative timing : 45 mins)

You are Terry Smith, a Management Accountant attached to a team responsible for the accountancy function of a group of companies. Together with your line manager you are responsible for designing and presenting accountancy training sessions for your team and throughout the organisation.

You receive the following email from your line manager, Gerald Downes.

From: Gerald Downes
To: Terry Smith
Sent: 10 October 20X5
Subject: Accountancy training

Dear Terry,

As you know, the date of the next quarterly training session is approaching, and I am making preparations for the event. I would like you to take a more prominent role in the proceedings, and to this end I have suggested below some questions on a selection of topics.

(1)   An assistant of mine has produced a piece of work for his study course and he has asked me to have a look at it. In this piece of work he gives the definition of a non-current asset as 'a physical asset of substantial cost, owned by the company, which will last longer than one year'. Please provide an explanation that I can give to my assistant detailing the weaknesses in his definition of non-current assets when compared to the International Accounting Standards Board's (IASB) view of assets.

(2)   IAS 8 *Accounting policies, changes in accounting estimates and errors* contains guidance on the use of accounting policies and accounting estimates.

      Explain the basis on which the management of an entity must select its accounting policies and distinguish, using an example, between changes in accounting policies and changes in accounting estimates.

(3)   The objective of IAS 10 *Events after the reporting period* is to prescribe the treatment of events that occur after an entity's reporting period has ended.

      Define the period to which IAS 10 relates and distinguish between adjusting and non-adjusting events.

(4)   (a)   Set out the exemptions from the requirement to present consolidated financial statements which are available to a parent company.

      (b)   Explain why intra-group transactions and balances are eliminated on consolidation.

If you could let me have your responses by email I can have a look at them before the training session.

Thanks in advance,

Gerald

Write your response to the email from Gerald

Task 22 - Madeira

(indicative timing : 45 mins)

The following information relates to a company called Madeira:

DRAFT STATEMENT OF PROFIT OR LOSS FOR THE YEAR ENDED 30 SEPTEMBER 20X5

	$'000
Revenue	58,500
Cost of sales	(46,500)
Gross profit	12,000
Operating expenses	(8,700)
Investment income	1,100
Finance costs	(500)
Profit before tax	3,900
Income tax expense	(1,000)
Profit for the year	2,900

You are Gemma Riley, a member of the management accounting team at Madeira.

You receive the following email from your line manager:

From: Evelyn Snow
To: Gemma Riley
Sent: 10 October 20X5
Subject: Statement of cash flows

Dear Gemma,

As you know, the finance team are currently busy preparing the financial statements for the year just ended. As part of this process I have asked one of our trainee accountants to prepare the draft statement of cash flows, and an extract is shown below:

MADEIRA'S STATEMENT OF CASH FLOWS FOR THE YEAR ENDED 30 SEPTEMBER 20X5

	$'000
Cash flows from operating activities	
Profit before taxation	3,900
Adjustments for	
Depreciation	(1,060)
Loss on sale of building	210
	3,050
Increase in inventories	(490)
Decrease in trade payables	290
Net cash from operating activities	2,850

I am due to run a training session on statements of cash flows for new members of the team, and I would like you to prepare some notes for me that I can use as part of the training. The notes should cover the following:

(1)   Explain the main benefits, to users of the accounts, of including a statement of cash flows in published financial statements.

(2)   Describe the three main headings used in a statement of cash flows according to IAS 7, and indicate under which heading the following would appear:

(i)   Tax paid
(ii)   Loss on disposal of machinery

(3)   Looking at the extract from the draft statement of cash flows shown above, explain what errors have been made in preparing it.

(4)   Shareholders can often be confused when trying to evaluate the information provided to them by a company's financial statements, particularly when comparing accruals-based information in the income statement and the statement of financial position with that in the statement of cash flows.

In the two areas stated below, illustrate how information in a statement of cash flows may give a different perspective of events than that given by accruals-based financial statements:

(i)   Operating performance
(ii)   Investment in property, plant and equipment

(5)   Which one of the following would be shown in a statement of cash flow using the direct method but not in a statement of cash flow using the indirect method of calculating cash generated from operations?

Cash payments to employees
Increase/(decrease) in receivables
Depreciation
Finance costs

Write your response to the email from Evelyn

Task 23 - Cash management

(indicative timing : 45 mins)

You are Alphonse Surinam, a trainee management accountant working for a company that manufactures and sells sports equipment and clothing. The company has a chain of shops and also sells its products to other retail outlets such as department stores and online traders.

Today is 30 April 20X4 and you receive the following email from the Director of Finance:

From: Emily Cross, Director of Finance
To: Alphonse Surinam, Management Accountant
Sent: 30 April 20X4
Subject: Cash management

Dear Alphonse,

I hope that you are settling into your new role, and that your training is progressing well.

Next week I am due to give a presentation at the Finance Team meeting, in order to provide some in-house training to some new members of staff who have recently joined the finance department.

To help me with this, I'd be grateful if you could write some notes for me that I can use in the presentation. The notes should address the following topics:

(1)   Discuss the significance of trade payables in a company's working capital cycle, and the dangers of over-reliance on trade credit as a source of finance.

(2)   Explain the possible benefits and limitations of a Just-In-Time (JIT) purchasing system.

(3)   Identify the services that may be provided by factoring organisations.

(4)   A company, when deciding its cash management policy, has to balance the costs of holding insufficient cash with the costs of holding cash. The motives for holding cash can be categorised as follows:

- Transaction motive
- Precautionary motive
- Speculative motive

Explain the three categories of motives for holding cash given above.

If you could let me have your responses, via email, by the end of the week, that will give me time to prepare my notes for the meeting.

Thank you and best regards,

Emily

Write your response to the email from Emily

Task 24 - Oland

(indicative timing : 45 mins)

After a recent financial crisis in the country of Oland, there had been a number of high profile company failures and a general loss of confidence in business. As a result, an updated corporate governance code was proposed, with changes to address these concerns.

Before the new code was published, there was a debate in Oland society about whether corporate governance provisions should be made rules-based, or remain principles-based as had been the case in the past. One elected legislator, Martin Mung, whose constituency contained a number of the companies that had failed with resulting rises in unemployment, argued strongly that many of the corporate governance failures would not have happened if directors were legally accountable for compliance with corporate governance provisions. He said that 'you can't trust the markets to punish bad practice', saying that this was what had caused the problems in the first place. He said that Oland should become a rules-based jurisdiction because the current 'comply or explain' was ineffective as a means of controlling corporate governance.

Mr Mung was angered by the company failures in his constituency and believed that a lack of sound corporate governance contributed to the failure of important companies and the jobs they supported. He said that he wanted the new code to make it more difficult for companies to fail.

The new code was then issued, under a principles-based approach. One added provision in the new Oland code was to recommend a reduction in the re-election period of all directors from three years to one year. The code also required that when seeking re-election, there should be 'sufficient biographical details on each director to enable shareholders to take an informed decision'. The code explained that these measures were 'in the interests of greater accountability'.

Martin Mung believes that Oland should become a rules-based jurisdiction because the current 'comply or explain' approach is ineffective as a means of controlling corporate governance.

Today is 10 October 20X5. You are Jane Weller, a trainee management accountant. You receive an email from your Anne Beenet, your head of department, following a team meeting during which corporate governance and the situation in Oland was discussed.

From: Anne Beenet, Head of Department
To: Jane Weller, Management Accountant
Sent: 10 October 20X5
Subject: Corporate Governance

Dear Jane,

I hope that you enjoyed the recent team meeting and that you found the discussion informative. As part of the follow up to the meeting I am putting together some background notes and would be glad of your assistance. I would like you to provide me with the following information:

(1)   Examine how sound corporate governance can make it more difficult for companies to fail, clearly explaining what 'corporate governance' means in your answer.

(2)   Explain the difference between rules-based and principles-based approaches to corporate governance regulation, and argue against Martin Mung's belief that 'comply or explain' is ineffective.

(3)   Explain what 'accountability' means, and discuss how the proposed new provisions for shorter re-election periods and biographical details might result in 'greater accountability' as the code suggests.

You can send me your responses in the form of an email, preferably by the end of the week.

Thank you and best regards,

Anne

Write your response to the email from Anne

Topic 5 – F1 Further Tasks Solutions

Task 19

Marking scheme

	Marks	Marks
Sub-task 1		
Defined contribution	5	
Defined benefit	5	
How accounted for in financial statements	5	
		15
Sub-task 2		
IAS 19 recognition		2
Sub-task 3		
Advantages of PAYE – 1 mark per point		3
Sub-task 4		
Tax avoidance	2½	
Tax evasion	2½	
		5
MAXIMUM FOR TASK		25

Suggested solution:

From:	Jem Owen
To:	Harry Broad
Sent:	10 October 20X5
Subject:	Pensions and taxation

Dear Harry,

Thank you for your email. Please see my responses below:

(1) Defined contribution

Under the defined contribution plan, JKL's legal or constructive **obligation is limited** to the amount that it agrees to contribute to the fund. Therefore, the employees bear the risks of the pension plan. In the statement of profit or loss and other comprehensive income within profit or loss, an **expense** should be recognised for the **contributions for the year** (regardless of whether or not they have been paid by JKL). In the statement of financial position, the difference between the contributions paid for the year and the expense in profit or loss, should be recorded as an **accrual** (if cash paid is less than the expense) or a prepayment (if cash paid is greater than the expense).

Defined benefit

Under the defined benefit scheme, JKL's employees are **guaranteed a fixed annual pension** based on their final salary and the number of years worked – for example, (final salary/60) × number of years worked. JKL must ensure that there are sufficient assets

169

available to pay the guaranteed pensions. If there is a deficit (insufficient assets to pay the liabilities), JKL must make good the deficit by increasing contributions. Equally, if there is a surplus (more assets than required to pay the liabilities), JKL will benefit from reduced contributions or a refund in the future. Therefore, **JKL takes on the risks and benefits on the pension plan** and must **recognise the pension plan's assets (at fair value) and liabilities (at present value)** in one line in their statement of financial position (with a breakdown of the movement for the year in the notes to the accounts). In the statement of profit or loss and other comprehensive income, JKL will recognise in profit or loss:

- **Current service cost** – the extra pension the employee is owed for working for another year

- **Past service cost** – change in the present value of plan liabilities resulting from a plan amendment or a curtailment

- **Net interest on the net defined benefit liability (asset)** – the change during the period in the net defined benefit liability (asset) that arises from the passage of time

In **other comprehensive income**, JKL should **recognise remeasurement (actuarial) gains or losses** arising on plan assets and liabilities in the year. The remeasurement gains or losses result from the year end actuarial valuation of plan assets and liabilities differing from the accounting values.

(2) An entity must recognise the remeasurement gains and losses **immediately in other comprehensive income.**

All other options were removed by the 2011 revision to IAS 19 *Employee benefits*.

(3) The advantages of a PAYE system from the point of view of the government are:

(a) Tax is deducted at source, so non-payment is not an issue
(b) The costs of collection are borne by employers
(c) The funds are received at the same time each month, which helps financial planning

(4) The company acts as a tax collector on behalf of the tax authority. Therefore any tax deducted is recorded in a payable account until the money is actually paid to the tax authority. The balance on the payable account represents the amount collected but not yet paid over.

(5) Tax avoidance is a way of arranging your affairs to take advantage of the tax rules to pay as little tax as possible. It is perfectly legal. Cee has avoided tax by taking expert tax advice and investing her money in a tax efficient way in order to pay less tax.

Tax evasion is a way of paying less tax by illegal methods, eg not declaring the income or money laundering. Gee has evaded tax by not declaring all the income he earns on his annual tax return and so reducing his tax bill.

I hope that these responses address your points adequately; if not please do not hesitate to contact me.

Regards,

Jem

Competency coverage

Sub-task	Technical		Business acumen		People		Leadership		Max
1	Definitions	10							15
	Accounting	5							
2	IAS 19	2							2
3	PAYE	3							3
4	Taxation	5							5
Total		25							25

This task requires technical knowledge of different types of pension plans, and how such plans are accounted for in the financial statements of an entity. There is also a need to demonstrate knowledge of IAS 19 and PAYE, and to be able to explain the difference between tax evasion and tax avoidance.

Task 20

Marking scheme

	Marks	Marks
Sub-task 1		
1 mark per valid point, up to a maximum of eight	8	
		8
Sub-task 2		
1 mark per valid point, up to a maximum of five	5	
		5
Sub-task 3		
Withholding tax – 1 mark per valid point, up to a maximum of two	2	
Double tax - 1 mark per valid point, up to a maximum of five	5	
Fraston - 1 mark per valid point, up to a maximum of five	5	
		12
MAXIMUM FOR TASK		25

Suggested solution:

From:	Clemy Hougton
To:	Javier Lupo
Sent:	31 August 20X2
Subject:	Group structure

As requested, please find my notes below:

(1) Control vs Significant Influence

Control is defined by IFRS 10 as follows: 'An investor controls an investee when the investor is **exposed**, or has rights, to **variable returns** from its involvement with the investee and has the **ability to affect those returns** through **power** over the investee'.

Control can usually be assumed to exist when the parent owns more than half (ie over 50%) of the voting power of an entity *unless* it can be clearly shown that such ownership does not constitute control, which is rare.

IFRS 10 states that an investor controls an investee only if all three of the following apply. The investor has:

(i) Power over the investee;

(ii) Exposure to, or rights to, variable returns from its involvement with the investee; and

(iii) The ability to use its power over the investee to affect the amount of the investor's returns.

Power may be obtained from direct ownership of voting rights or may be derived from other rights, such as the right to appoint and remove key personnel.

Significant influence is the power to participate in decisions in the entity, but does not constitute control.

Significant influence can usually be determined by the holding of voting rights in the entity, generally in the form of shares. Where an investor holds between 20% and 50% of the voting power in an entity, it can be presumed that the investor holds significant influence over the entity, unless it can be clearly shown that this is not the case.

Significant influence may take various forms:

(i)   Participation in the policy making process
(ii) Material transactions between investee and investor
(iii) Board representation
(iv) Provision of technical advice
(v)   An interchange of personnel between the companies

(2)   Augusta

At 31 March 20X1 Paladin could be presumed to have 'significant influence' over Augusta arising from its 25% shareholding. Augusta was therefore treated as an associate and its results were brought into Paladin's financial statements using the equity method.

Spekulate's purchase of 65% changes Paladin's position. Spekulate now has control, so Paladin can no longer be regarded as having significant influence. This is illustrated by the fact that Paladin has lost its seat on the board. Paladin's investment in Augusta should be treated in 20X2 under IFRS 9, carried at fair value, with any gains or losses taken to profit or loss.

(3)   Tax

(a)   Withholding tax

If a company makes payments to an individual or another company resident in a different tax jurisdiction, it may have to pay withholding tax to the tax authority of its own jurisdiction.

The reason for this is to ensure that the local government of the country in which the foreign company is resident earns some tax revenue from the payment of money abroad, so that not all of the profits of the company is remitted overseas (in the form of dividends, interest or royalty, for example). Therefore, the local tax authority will deduct at source a withholding tax from certain types of payments sent abroad. The rate of withholding tax varies depending upon the country's tax regime, and the existence of double taxation treaties.

(b)   Double tax

A company is taxed in the country where it is resident in for tax purposes. Tax residence can be determined in different ways in different jurisdictions, so that a company may find itself deemed to be resident in two different countries. For example, if a company is legally incorporated in one country, but has its place of effective management in another country, it may be deemed resident in both countries and its income may be taxed in both countries – ie it may suffer double taxation.

Countries need double taxation agreements to determine which country should tax a company's income in this kind of situation. Double taxation agreements also specify what kind of reliefs are available to companies who have a taxable presence in more than one country.

Methods of giving relief

One way is to give full deduction for foreign taxes paid. However, this is not always appropriate, particularly if the country where the tax is paid has a high tax rate and the other has a low rate.

Relief may be given by exemption. In this case, if income is taxed in Country A, then it will not be taxed in Country B.

Another way of giving relief is by credit. Under this system, the tax already paid in Country A is deducted from the tax due in Country B. Note that no refund of tax is given if the tax paid in Country A is higher than the tax due in Country B.

(c) Fraston

Fraston's production facility and head office are located in Germany and all the directors' board meetings are held in Germany, so its effective management is in Germany.

France and Germany have a double tax treaty with each other based on the OECD Model Tax Convention, so the OECD Model Tax Convention will apply to Fraston. Where an entity is deemed to be taxable in several countries, the OECD Model Tax Convention suggests that the entity is resident in the country of its effective management. Fraston will therefore be regarded as resident in Germany for tax purposes and will be taxable in Germany.

The OECD Model Tax Convention states that an entity's profits will only be taxed in a country if the entity has a permanent establishment in the country.

Fraston has an office in France, providing services to customers and selling Fraston's products. The OECD Model Tax Convention states that a branch office is likely to constitute a permanent establishment, so Fraston will likely have a permanent establishment in France. If this is the case, profits made by Fraston's branch office in France will be taxable in France

As Fraston is resident in Germany, its worldwide profits will be taxed in Germany, irrespective of where they arise.

As the countries have a double tax treaty with each other, Fraston should be able to obtain relief for any tax paid in France under the double taxation agreement.

I hope that this is helpful,

Clemy

Competency coverage

Sub-task	Technical		Business acumen		People		Leadership		Max
1	Groups - control	8							8
2	Accounting treatment	5							5
3	Withholding tax	2							12
	Double tax - explanation	5							
	Double tax - evaluation	5							
Total		25							25

This task requires knowledge of groups, especially what constitutes control. There is also a section on tax in an international environment. All of the sub-tasks come under technical competence.

Task 21

Marking scheme

	Marks	Marks
Sub-task 1		
Conceptual framework definition	1	
1 mark per explanation of differences	4	
		5
Sub-task 2		
1 mark per valid point		5
Sub-task 3		
Definition	1	
Discussion of adjusting events	2	
Reference to going concern	1	
Discussion on non-adjusting events	1	
		5
Sub-task 4		
(a) 1 mark per valid point up to a maximum of	5	
(b) 1 mark per valid point up to a maximum of	5	
		10
MAXIMUM FOR TASK		25

Suggested solution:

> From: Terry Smith
> To: Gerald Downes
> Sent: 10 October 20X5
> Subject: Accountancy training

Dear Gerald,

Thank you for your email regarding the forthcoming training session. I provide responses to your points below.

(1) The IASB *Conceptual Framework* defines an asset as 'a resource controlled by the entity as a result of past events and from which future economic benefits are expected to flow to the entity'. IAS 1 sets out the defining features of a current asset (intended to be realised during the normal operating cycle or within 12 months of the year end, held for trading or classified as cash or a cash equivalent). All other assets are classified as non-current.

Your assistant's definition diverges from this in a number of ways:

(i) A non-current asset does not have to be physical. The definition can include intangible assets such as investments or capitalised development costs.

(ii) A non-current asset does not have to be of substantial cost. An item of immaterial value is unlikely to be capitalised, but this is not part of the definition.

(iii) A non-current asset does not have to be legally owned. The accounting principle is based on 'substance over form' and relies on the ability of the entity to **control** the asset. This means for instance that an asset held under a finance lease is treated as an asset by the lessee, not the lessor.

(iv) It is generally the case that non-current assets will last longer than one year. IAS 16 specifies that property, plant and equipment 'are expected to be used during more than one period'. However, if a non-current asset failed to last longer than one year, it would **still be classified as a non-current asset during its life**.

(2) IAS 8 *Accounting policies, changes in accounting estimates and errors* requires an entity to determine the accounting policy to apply to a transaction or event by reference to any IFRS specifically applying to that transaction or event. Where there is no specific IFRS applicable, management is expected to **use its judgement** in applying an accounting policy which will result in information which is relevant and reliable. In this they should consider the requirements and guidance in IFRSs dealing with similar and related issues and also the *Conceptual Framework* definitions, recognition criteria and measurement concepts for assets, liabilities, income and expenses.

Accounting policies are the specific principles, bases and rules applied in measuring and presenting financial information. **Changes of accounting policy are not very common**. One example would be a change from the FIFO method of valuing inventory to the weighted average method – this is a change in the basis of valuation.

A **change of accounting estimate** is a change in the way in which these principles and bases are applied which leads to an adjustment to any of the elements identified by the *Conceptual Framework* – assets, liabilities, income or expenses. One example would be a change from the straight line method of depreciation to the reducing balance method. In this case the accounting policy is that non-current assets are carried at cost less accumulated depreciation, the accounting estimate is how that depreciation is calculated.

(3) IAS 10 relates to events taking place between the last day of the reporting period (the year end date) and the date on which the financial statements are approved and signed by the directors. This period is usually several months.

Adjusting events are events taking place after the reporting period which provide further evidence of conditions existing at the end of the reporting period or which call into question the going concern status of the entity. For this reason, adjusting events require adjustment to be made to the financial statements. If going concern is no longer applicable, the financial statements must be prepared on a break-up basis.

Non-adjusting events provide evidence of conditions arising **after** the end of the reporting period. If material, these should be disclosed by note, but they do not require that the financial statements be adjusted.

(4) (a) A parent need not present consolidated financial statements if one of the following exemptions applies.

- It is itself a wholly or partly-owned subsidiary of another entity and its other owners do not object to it not preparing consolidated financial statements.

- Its shares or debt instruments are not traded on any stock exchange.

- Its financial statements are not being filed with any regulatory organisation for the purpose of issuing any debt or equity instruments on any stock exchange.

- Its ultimate or any intermediate parent produces publicly-available financial statements that comply with IFRS.

(b) IFRS 10 requires intragroup balances, transactions, income and expenses to be eliminated in full. The purpose of consolidated financial statements is to present the financial position of the parent and subsidiaries as that of a **single entity**, the group. This means that, in the consolidated statement of profit or loss, the only profits recognised should be those earned by the group in trading with entities outside the group. Similarly, inventory should be valued at cost to the group.

When a company sells goods to another company in the same group it will recognise revenue and profit in its individual financial statements. However, from the point of view of the group, no sale has taken place, because the goods are still held by the group. The sale must therefore be eliminated from revenue and the unrealised profit must be eliminated from group inventory.

Where one group company owes money to another group company or one group company holds debt instruments issued by another company, the asset and liability balances will be eliminated on consolidation. As far as the group is concerned, they do not represent amounts due to or from third parties.

Please let me know if I can help with anything else,

Terry

Competency coverage

Sub-task	Technical		Business acumen	People		Leadership		Max
1	Conceptual framework	1						5
	Definitions	4						
2	IAS 8	5						5
3	IAS 10	5						5
4	IFRS 10	10						10
Total		25						25

This task covers a number of accounting standards and the conceptual framework. Students need to demonstrate a good technical knowledge of some of the key standards and concepts contained in the F1 syllabus.

Task - 22

Marking scheme

	Marks	Marks
Sub-task 1		
1 mark per well-made point up to a maximum of		5
Sub-task 2		
2 marks per sub-heading up to a maximum of		5
Sub-task 3		
2 ½ per error correctly identified		5
Sub-task 4		
Operating performance	2½	
Investment in PPE	2½	
		5
Sub-task 5		
Explanation		<u>5</u>
MAXIMUM FOR TASK		<u><u>25</u></u>

Suggested solution:

From:	Gemma Riley
To:	Evelyn Snow
Sent:	10 October 20X5
Subject:	Statement of cash flows

Dear Evelyn,

Thank you for your email. Please see below my response to each of your points in turn.

(1)   The statements of cash flows is used very much in conjunction with the rest of the financial statements. It enables the users of the financial statements to understand the change in net assets, of the entity's financial position (liquidity and solvency) and the entity's ability to adapt to changing circumstances by affecting the amount and timing of cash flows.

Statements of cash flows enhance comparability as they are not affected by differing accounting policies used for the same types of transactions or events.

Cash flow information of a historical nature can be used as an indicator of the amount, timing and certainty of future cash flows. Past forecast cash flow information can be checked for accuracy as actual figures emerge. The relationship between profit and cash flows can be analysed as can changes in prices over time.

(2) The three main headings used in a statement of cash flows are:

Cash flows from operating activities

This is perhaps the key part of the statement of cash flows because it shows whether, and to what extent, companies can generate cash from their operations. It is these operating cash flows which must, in the end, pay for all cash outflows relating to other activities, ie paying loan interest, dividends and so on.

Most of the components of cash flows from operating activities will be those items which determine the net profit or loss of the entity, ie they relate to the main revenue-producing activities of the entity.

Cash flows from investing activities

The cash flows classified under this heading show the extent of new investment in assets which will generate future profit and cash flows.

Cash flows from financing activities

This section of the statement of cash flows shows the share of cash which the entity's capital providers have claimed during the period. This is an indicator of likely future interest and dividend payments.

Tax paid and loss from disposal of machinery would be included under the heading "Cash flows from operating activities".

(3) The following errors have been made in the extract shown:

(i)   Depreciation should have been added, not deducted.
(ii) Decrease in trade payables should have been deducted, not added.

(4) (i)   The statement of profit or loss of Madeira shows profit for the year of $3.9 million. However, this figure includes amounts based on estimates, such as depreciation, which do not result in a movement of cash.

Net cash from operating activities records only those transactions which have resulted in movements of cash, so items which rely on judgement or are unrealised are automatically excluded. It is, to this degree, a more verifiable amount than profit before tax and many users would consider it more useful.

(ii) Accrual-based financial information spreads the lives of property, plant and equipment over the periods expected to benefit from their use and this can be affected by revaluations, impairment and changes in expected life, which are all issues based on judgement. Also, entities can choose whether or not to transfer back excess depreciation to retained earnings following a revaluation. So there is a lot of subjectivity involved in asset values.

Net cash from investing activities deals simply in amounts paid to acquire property, plant and equipment and in any proceeds of selling property, plant and equipment. This is valuable and verifiable additional information which is not shown by the statement of financial position.

(5)   Cash payments to employees would be shown in a statement of cash flows prepared using the direct method, but not in a statement of cashflows prepared using the indirect method. The direct method discloses the major classes of gross cash receipts and cash payments. The indirect method calculates the net cash position by making adjustments to the net profit or loss..

Please do not hesitate to get in touch again if I can be of any further assistance with your presentation.

Best regards,

Gemma

Competency coverage

Sub-task	Technical		Business acumen		People		Leadership		Max
1	Benefits of statement of cash flows	5							5
2	Statement of cash flows headings	5							5
3	Errors	5							5
4	SCF/SPL – performance	2½							5
	SCF/SPL – PPE	2½							
5	Direct method	5							5
Total		25							25

This task concentrates on one of the key financial statements and tests students' knowledge of what the statement contains and why it is useful. It also tests the preparation of one of the sections of the statement, using an extract that has been prepared with some errors in it. All of this task relies on technical knowledge.

Task 23

Marking scheme

	Marks	Marks
Sub-task 1		
Trade payables in working capital cycle	5	
Over-reliance on trade credit	5	
		10
Sub-task 2		
Benefits of JIT		
		5
Sub-task 3		
1 mark per valid point, up to a maximum of		5
Sub-task 4		
1 mark per valid point, up to a maximum of		5
MAXIMUM FOR TASK		25

Suggested solution:

From:	Alphonse Surinam
To:	Emily Cross
Sent:	30 April 20X4
Subject:	Cash management

Dear Emily,

Thank you for your email; please see below my responses to each of your points in turn:

(1) **Trade payables and trade credit**

(i) <u>Working capital management</u>

The net working capital of a business can be defined as its current assets less its current liabilities. The management of working capital is concerned with ensuring that sufficient liquid resources are maintained within the business. For the majority of businesses, particularly manufacturing businesses, trade payables will form the major part of the current liabilities figure.

<u>Trade credit period</u>

It follows that the trade credit period taken will be a major determinant of the working capital requirement of the company. This is calculated (in days) as the total value of trade payables divided by the level of credit purchases × 365.

<u>Cash conversion cycle</u>

A link can be made between working capital and liquidity by means of the cash conversion cycle. This measures the length of time that elapses between a firm paying for its various purchases and receiving payment for its sales. It can be

calculated as the receivable days plus the inventory period less the trade credit period, and it measures the length of time for which net current assets must be financed.

(ii) <u>Use of trade credit</u>

For many firms, trade payables provide a very important source of short-term credit. Since very few companies currently impose interest charges on overdue accounts, taking extended credit can appear to be a very cheap form of short-term finance. However, such a policy entails some risks and costs that are not immediately apparent, as follows.

(a) If discounts are being forgone, the effective cost of this should be evaluated – it may be more beneficial to shorten the credit period and take the discounts.

(b) If the company gains a reputation for slow payment this will damage its credit standing, making it difficult to obtain credit from new suppliers in the future.

(c) Suppliers who are having to wait for their money may seek recompense in other ways, for example by raising prices or by placing a lower priority on new orders. Such actions could do damage to both the efficiency and profitability of the company.

(d) Suppliers may place the company 'on stop' until the account is paid. This can jeopardise supplies of essential raw materials which in turn could cause production to stop: this will result in a high level of unwanted costs, damaging the company's reputation.

(2) **Just-in-time (JIT) purchasing system**

<u>Benefits</u>

Possible benefits of a JIT purchasing system are as follows.

(i) Reduction of inventory holding costs.
(ii) Reduced manufacturing lead times.

<u>Limitations</u>

A JIT purchasing system has the following limitations.

(i) Not always appropriate. For example, running out of inventory in a hospital could prove fatal.

(ii) Large up-front costs of a full study of production methods.

(iii) Access to sizeable funds is required to run a JIT purchasing system.

<u>Alternative Answers</u>

We have given five points here as the question is for five marks. You would also have scored marks for the following.

<u>Benefits</u>

- Improved labour productivity.
- Reduced scrap/rework/warrant costs.
- Higher quality products, resulting in improved customer satisfaction.

- Increased flexibility to supply small batches as production matches ultimate demand.
- May help with the identification of weaknesses such as unreliable suppliers.

Limitations

- A JIT purchasing system requires long-term commitment to suppliers and so reduces flexibility in supplier choice.

- For JIT to work, suppliers must be able to regularly deliver materials of appropriate quality on time and at short notice.

(3) **Services provided by factoring organisations**

A factor normally manages the debts owed to a client on the client's behalf

Services provided by factoring organisations

(i) Administration of the client's invoicing, sales accounting and debt collection.

(ii) Credit protection for the client's debts, whereby the factor takes over the risk of loss from irrecoverable debts and so 'insures' the client against such losses. The factor may purchase these debts 'without recourse' to the client, which means that if the client's customers do not pay what they owe, the factor will not ask for the money back from the client.

(iii) 'Factor finance' may be provided, the factor advancing cash to the client against outstanding debts. The factor may advance up to 85% of approved debts from the date of invoice.

(iv) A confidentiality agreement may be offered to conceal the existence of the arrangement from customers.

(4) **Motives for holding cash**

Transactions motive

Cash is needed for every-day expenses such as wages and payments to suppliers.

This is particularly important for seasonal businesses.

Precautionary motive

This is cash held 'just in case' to cover unexpected expenditure, for example, unexpected material price rises or a labour strike.

Not having enough cash can lead to loss of settlement discounts, loss of goodwill, bank fees and in some cases, failure of the business.

Speculative motive

This is cash held to take advantage of any unforeseen profit-making opportunities. For example, taking advantage of unexpected early repayment discounts.

I hope that the above responses provide you with the information you need for your presentation. If I can be of any further assistance please let me know.

Regards,

Alphonse

Competency coverage

Sub-task	Technical		Business acumen		People		Leadership		Max
1	Trade payables	5							10
	Trade credit	5							
2	JIT	5							5
3	Factoring	5							5
4	Cash holding	5							5
Total		25							25

This task tests a student's knowledge of working capital management.

Task 24

Marking scheme

	Marks	Marks
Sub-task 1		
Explanation of corporate governance	2	
2 marks for each point on corporate governance and failure	10	
Maximum		10
Sub-task 2		
Distinguish between rules- and principles-based approaches	2	
2 marks for each point on comply or explain	6	
		8
Sub-task 3		
Accountability	2	
2 marks for each relevant discussion point on greater accountability	7	
Maximum		7
MAXIMUM FOR TASK		25

Suggested solution:

From: Jane Weller
To: Anne Beenet
Sent: 10 October 20X5
Subject: Corporate governance

Dear Anne,

Thank you for your email. Please find my responses below:

(1)   **Definition of corporate governance**

Corporate governance is the system by which companies are **directed and controlled.** It focuses on the relationships between a company's directors, shareholders and other stakeholders. It provides the structure through which the **objectives of the company** are **set**, and the **means of achieving those objectives and monitoring performance** are **determined**.

Promotion of relationships with shareholders

Good governance should ensure alignment of the **interests of shareholders and directors**. It should minimise the chances of agency problems arising through directors pursuing their own interests and **threatening the company's future** by **reckless behaviour**, or failing to pursue the best long-term strategies for the company.

Risk management

If a company is to achieve its objectives, it must have systems in place for the **identification, evaluation and mitigation** of risk. These systems should particularly

186

highlight risks that may have serious impacts upon the future of the company, so that effective action can be taken to deal with them.

Control systems

As part of risk management good governance should ensure that **effective controls** that protect the business are being operated. These include controls that ensure that business assets are being **safeguarded** and resources are **not being wasted on unprofitable activities,** but are being used efficiently and effectively.

Promotes reporting

A well-governed company will demonstrate transparency by providing financial information that is **accurate and fair** and also additional, voluntary, disclosures. These will help investors and other key stakeholders make informed decisions about the company. Full disclosure will also encourage **accountability**, as directors and senior managers will know that stakeholders have the **information available to scrutinise their stewardship effectively**.

Promotes stakeholder confidence

If a company is believed to be well-governed, then those who deal with it can have **trust** in their relationships with it. It is particularly important for shareholders to have confidence, as a loss of belief will lead to the company's market price falling, maybe threatening its future. There are also other important stakeholders, such as taxation authorities or industry regulators, who can be a serious threat to companies that they do not believe to be sound and therefore take action against them.

Attracts funding

Good governance can be a means of **attracting additional funding** into a company. More sources of funds may be available and the **costs** of different sources of funds could be **lower**. This should enhance solvency as more cash will be available over the longer-term, and liquidity, as fixed finance costs should be low.

(2) **Difference between rules-based and principles-based approaches**

A rules-based approach emphasises **definite, measurable actions**. It does not judge a company by underlying issues which cannot be the subject of regulation. Compliance with the rules is **compulsory and enforceable in law**. Penalties will be imposed on companies that break the rules. A principles-based approach is also not optional, but **compliance is enforced by stock market or investor pressure**, not legal sanctions. A principles-based approach emphasises the **achievement of objectives** and accepts the possibility that different actions may be equally effective in achieving the desired objectives.

Arguments against Martin Mung's belief

Circumstances of non-compliance

Martin Mung's belief appears to be based on the view that companies can ignore the requirements of principles-based codes. This is not true. As explained above, markets and investors generally **expect compliance**. Non-compliance should mostly occur in unusual circumstances or transitional situations, for example an unforeseen, sudden, change in a board of directors.

Appropriateness of response

Principles based codes also allow companies to develop approaches that are the most **appropriate and cost-effective** for their own circumstances. There may be specific reasons why a particular company may not comply with what would often be regarded as governance best practice.

Enforcement of transparency

'Comply or explain' requires companies to provide reasons for, and full details of, areas of non-compliance with the code. This **enhances transparency.** Full disclosure enables investors and others to make an **informed judgement** on whether they accept the reasons for non-compliance.

Market reaction

Real-life experience suggests that markets will not simply allow bad behaviour. Significant institutional investors in particular can put considerable pressure on companies by selling shares, raising issues at general meetings or direct intervention. They have a strong motivation for **protecting the value** of their investment. They will also wish to gain assurance that **non-compliance** has been **resolved**, rather than just enforcing punishments on companies that have broken the rules.

Legislation may be ineffective

By emphasising principles, a 'comply or explain' approach may **ensure wider compliance** than a rules-based approach. There have been several instances of companies failing who fulfilled the accounting regulations in force at the time, but nevertheless failed to report accurately and fairly as would be required by a principles-based approach.

(3) **Accountability**

Accountability refers to whether a **company and its directors** can be held **answerable** for their actions, particularly to shareholders as directors are shareholders' **agents**. The measures proposed aim to give shareholders greater power to make directors answerable and to **impose their will upon boards**.

Impact of new proposals

Removal of underperforming directors

Making re-election compulsory every year gives investors the chance to **remove under-performing directors quickly**. Directors will be aware that their achievements will be judged every year by investors and that they do not have the right to remain on the board. However, there is a risk that directors' performance will be considered solely on the basis of the results of the last year, and that investors will be less focused on judging how directors have ensured longer-term success.

Directors' rewards

There will also be **compatibility** between the period for which directors' remuneration is assessed and the period over which investors judge directors' performance. Making annual re-election compulsory should also remove the need to compensate directors for loss of office. Directors will simply not be re-elected, rather than having their contracts terminated prematurely and being able to seek compensation.

Evolution of board

Annual re-election allows for more **rapid changes in the composition of the board**. If shareholders feel that the board collectively has become complacent and less in-touch with shareholder requirements, they can alter its composition quickly. It also gives shareholders greater opportunity to promote changes in the underlying characteristics of the board as a whole, for example making the board more diverse.

Biographical details

Publication of details of potential directors should enable shareholders to make an informed judgement about whether they have the **knowledge and experience** necessary to make an **effective contribution** to the board. Once directors have been elected, shareholders may be able to judge whether the contribution that they appear to have made seems to be in line with what they could have been expected to do.

I hope that this provides you with the information you need to prepare your notes. If I can be of help with anything else please let me know.

Kind regards,

Jane

Competency coverage

Sub-task	Technical		Business acumen	People		Leadership		Max
1			Corporate governance CG and failure	10				10
2			Rules and principles	8				8
3			Accountability	7				7
Total				25				25

This task is designed to show that the student has business acumen and understands the importance of corporate governance.

Topic 6 – E1 Task Practice

Topic 6 – E1 Primary Tasks

Task 25 - LD2

(indicative timing : 45 minutes)

The LD2 group was established as a family-run business supplying kitchens to the general public over 25 years ago. They gained a reputation locally for their high quality finishes and hands-on project management, ensuring all jobs ran to the time scales specified by the client. Although the group remains in family ownership, as the original board members retire from their operational roles, they have been replaced with an ambitious senior management team. However, the original board members still remain active at board meetings.

The latest recruit was the new Managing Director, Bob Carter, who has grown LD2 rapidly over the past five years through acquiring a number of smaller kitchen accessory manufacturers and kitchen suppliers and fitters. As a consequence of this strategy LD2 has 'inherited' many different systems, many manual and paper-based, which it has continued to operate. LD2's technology now lags far behind that of its competitors, many of whom are experimenting with online trading.

Today is 12th May 20X5

You have just received the following extract from the board meeting minutes from 5th May 20X5:

LD2

Meeting Minutes: 5th May 20X5
Next meeting: 5th June 20X5

A number of quality and other problems within the group have now become apparent including:

- Incompatibility of software
- Complex reconciliation of systems output being performed
- Stock shortages leading to contract delays
- Late management reports, and
- Payroll and invoicing errors due to faulty data entry and calculation.

Bob Carter has raised concerns that these problems are beginning to tarnish the reputation and brand image of LD2. He now wants to consolidate the business by simplifying and improving the quality of its operations. A budget has been proposed to introduce a quality approach, renew equipment and standardise systems.

The Board agreed for the need to establish a working group to develop solutions and bring about improvements.

Subsequent to the Board meeting held on 5th May 20X5,a working group has been established and the first workshop was held on 8th May 20X5.

This morning, Bob Carter sent you the following e-mail:

From: Bob Carter BC@LD2.co.uk
To: Sarah Walker SW@LD2.co.uk
Sent: 12th May 20X5, 10.27am
Subject: New ERP system

Sarah,

At the Board meeting last week, it was agreed that in order to maintain our brand image, we need to consolidate LD2 by simplifying and improving the quality of its operations.

A working group has already been established and prepared the following general systems recommendations:

- Introduce a single Enterprise Resource Planning (ERP) system for the whole group. A leading supplier in the Industry has been preliminarily selected. This will enable real-time data sharing between the factory, warehouse and purchasing teams. Also within this system a web browser would allow managers to have immediate access to information on diaries, overtime, holidays and sickness, as well as being able to submit accurate timesheet entries directly into a central payroll system;

- Engage a specialist to develop a corporate website comparable to the best in the industry.

As you are aware, my background is in sales and I have to admit that I understand very little about the role you perform as the Management Accountant responsible for reconciling the current systems. This afternoon, I need to prepare a report for the next board meeting to justify the anticipated expenditure of such a project and gain agreement from the shareholders before we commit to it.

It would be very useful for me if you could send me an email that explains:

- How the ERP system could help LD2

- Any privacy and security issues that may need to be considered

- The likely features of the proposed corporate website if it is to be comparable to the best in the industry

I also recall that in your last role you were involved in a project to introduce a new computer system. Your recommendation on the most suitable change over method would be very useful.

Many thanks,
Bob

Bob Carter
Managing Director, LD2

Write your response to the email from Bob Carter

Task 26 - 2JN

(indicative timing : 45 minutes)

2JN is a large white goods manufacturing organisation which is structured with a number of supervisors each responsible for their own work production unit. Each factory consists of a number of work production units: Goods Inwards, Assembly, Paint Shop, Quality Control, Packing and Finished Goods stores. Supervisors report to a team of senior managers who in turn are accountable to John Ireland, the Managing Director. Performance is measured in terms of units produced per shift and department cost per full time equivalent (i.e. per head of employee). Operations are supported by 2JN's own finance, sales, distribution and human resource units.

Within the past two years, Martin Warwick, the Operations Director, has implemented a series of initiatives aimed at reducing product defects and customer complaints. The initiatives have included the appointment of a few quality control inspectors to support supervisors. Despite these efforts, 2JN has lost some of its major customers to its competitors and its profits aredeclining.2JN's operations were originally designed 30 years ago and during this time, as new machinery was introduced it was installed wherever there was space. This means work in progress needs to be moved across the factory several times during the production process. This can sometimes lead to damage and the need for re-work. The flow of operations around the factory requires urgent attention.

After discussions with customers and suppliers, John has discovered that other companies within the same industry have successfully adopted a Total Quality Management (TQM) approach. At a recent senior management meeting he announced that a TQM programme would be introduced within 2JN as a matter of priority.

Today is 7ᵗʰ May 20X5

You have just received the following extract from the board meeting minutes from 5ᵗʰ May 20X5:

2JN

Meeting Minutes: 5ᵗʰ May 20X5
Next meeting: 5ᵗʰ June 20X5

A benchmarking exercise was presented by Martin Warwick, revealing that 2JN's costs of production are much higher than those of its competitors. In addition, innovations in operations theory and techniques such as those in supply chain management and process design have not been seized. Clearly this needs addressing.

John Ireland announced that a TQM programme would be introduced within 2JN as a matter of priority. To support this, a Quality Committee will be established to oversee the programme's introduction and operation. He has tasked Pat Barnes, as the Human Resource Director, to establish Quality Circles to meet on a regular basis and arrange training in TQM for all staff. John concluded by saying that TQM was vital to 2JN and that high quality 'will both put costs down and revenue up'.

This morning, Martin Warwick sent you the following e-mail:

From: Martin Warwick MW@2JN.co.uk
To: Andy Barker AB@2JN.co.uk
Sent: 7th May 20X5, 09.25am
Subject: TQM Requirements

Andy,

At our monthly management account review meeting last week, you mentioned that you had been studying theories of supply chain management as part of your CIMA studies. As you may be aware, John has announced the introduction of a Total Quality Management (TQM) programme, and tasked Pat with setting up and training quality circles.

Having worked at 2JN for the last 20 years, I have not seen such programmes in practice and would like to learn more to ensure the implementation is successful. In particular, I am concerned that the regular quality circle meetings and focus on Quality will increase cost of operations. Please could you provide me with some information that I could use for a presentation I am giving to the factory supervisors this afternoon:

- Explain the requirements for achieving a Total Quality Management (TQM) approach within 2JN.

- Identify the important issues and work groups that need to be considered when organising the TQM training in 2JN.

- Discuss the claim that high quality 'will both put costs down and revenue up'.

- With reference to Business Process Re-engineering (BPR) and process maps (or charts), explain how process design could assist 2JN to improve its competitive performance.

Many thanks,
Martin

Martin Warwick
Operations Director, 2JN

Write your response to the email from Martin Warwick

Task 27 - TB

(indicative timings : 45 minutes)

TB is a successful international telecommunication company with over 100,000 employees and a headquarters in its base country's capital city, Central. The headquarters staff include 10,000 employees in Finance, Information Systems (IS) and Human Resource (HR)) There is a sales function and a purchasing function in each of the global regions, North, South, East and West. Many corporate clients require on-site network support for their multi-site operations.

Industry regulators recently published a report that concluded successful telecommunications companies seized the opportunities of globalisation through a series of initiatives including using virtual work teams spread across continents, cultures and time zones. These initiatives helped to improve staff productivity and maximised the use of technology. Felicity Fox, the Finance Director, joined the Board of TB 6 months ago and is keen to use this new insight to drive business change and improvements at TB.

Today is 1st May 20X5

You have just received the following extract from the board meeting minutes from 28th April 20X5:

TB

Meeting Minutes: 28th April 20X5
Next meeting: 26th May 20X5

A review of the latest industry report has indicated a need for telecommunications companies to seize the opportunities of globalisation to remain successful in such a highly competitive environment. Felicity Fox has suggested using some of the key findings of this report to improve TB's operation. These include:

- Achieving fast communication and saving some travel costs through email, videoconferencing technology and Voip (voice over internet protocol) combined with webcam equipment;

- Improve communication through TB's own social networking sites with blogs, wikis, podcasts, RSS feeds and the use of instant messaging software;

- Offering a scheme of flexible working practices and home-working to TB headquarters staff.

Subsequent to the Board meeting held on 28th April 20X5,the board have proposed asking those switching to home working to 'give back' 50% of the time they previously spent commuting in the form of extra working hours. (The industry report estimates that home-workers get 20% more work done than those based in company offices and have comparatively lower absence and staff turnover levels.)

This morning, Felicity Fox sent you the following e-mail:

From: Felicity Fox FF@TB.co.uk
To: Sally Cooper SC@TB.co.uk
Sent: 1st May 20X5, 08.45am
Subject: Home Working Proposal

Sally,

I am in meetings all morning, but have agreed to do a presentation to the HR Director and HR Managers to highlight the key changes being proposed by introducing a voluntary move to home working for our head office staff. I will not have much time to put the presentation together, so I need you to help me with the main discussion points. Please send these over to me in an email by mid-morning. You need to make sure you cover the following areas:

- Explain the ways in which managers with responsibility for teams might meet the challenges of teams being geographically dispersed.

- Describe the advantages AND disadvantages of home-working for TB's headquarters staff.

- Describe the role that the HR department of TB can play given TB's proposed homeworking working practices.

Many thanks,
Felicity

Felicity Fox
Finance Director, TB

Write your response to the email from Felicity

Task 28 - 99

(indicative timing : 45 minutes)

Four years ago, Eric Winter retired as Financial Director of an airport company to become an ethical entrepreneur. He now employs ten people producing natural spring water and selling it in both still and sparkling varieties in individually sized plastic bottles. There has been no staff turnover whatsoever. The company, called 99, uses 'green' electricity and all profits go to a charity that installs pumps to provide clean water to some of the poorest communities in the world. Thanks to Eric's business contacts, 99's water is sold in a few garages, on airplane flights and in airport shops.

He has, however, found it impossible to get its water stocked by supermarkets because they want to charge a standard 'joining fee' for small suppliers, even though they know that 99 exists for charitable purposes. Despite this, and the fact that competition in the industry is intense, 99 has achieved rapid growth and significant profits (Eric receives no salary and the wages of employees are modest). Every time 99 sells enough bottles to build a new pump, it sends two employees abroad to help with the installation and pictures are published on the company website.

Last year Eric turned down a financially lucrative offer to sell 99 to a leading drinks company, believing that it did not really share his vision and was merely attempting to buy credibility with the growing number of consumers with ethical concerns. Now Zero, a large food and drinks company has made a similar offer.

Zero sees the acquisition of 99 as a way of complementing its product portfolio and furthering its marketing strategy of addressing consumers concerned about green and ethical issues. Zero, which began as a workers' cooperative, makes charitable donations annually, has carbon labelling on all of its products and has plans to make all packaging biodegradable or recyclable.

Today is 22nd May 20X5

You have just received the following extract from the board meeting minutes from 20th May 20X5:

Meeting Minutes: 20th May 20X5
Next meeting: 17th June 20X5

Eric presented a company review of Zero, including highlighting the main benefits that, by agreeing a deal with Zero, 99 would gain. The key points raised:

- Zero's distribution involves the use of low-carbon vehicles. This would provide 99 with an improved distribution network and environmentally cleaner transport.

- Should the takeover go through, Zero promises to operate at a distance, allowing 99 to run in a similar way.

- Zero promises to increase the current level of water pumps financed incrementally every year to double the numbers within the next five years.

- The opportunity to ensure bottles and packaging become 100% biodegradable or recyclable.

- Utilise Zero's expertise to develop the 99 brand still further

- An ability to get 99's water onto supermarket shelves

Subsequent to the Board meeting held on 20th May 20X5, a recent national survey has been published indicating that customers want products supplied and marketed responsibly and blame large retailers for not providing more environmentally and socially friendly products. Three quarters of respondents in the survey say that they 'completely agree' that they would choose a socially and environmentally responsible product over one that was not, and two thirds say that they would work for an ethical employer even if it meant being paid less.

This morning, Eric sent you the following e-mail:

From:	Eric Winter EW@99.co.uk
To:	Alex Summer AS@99.co.uk
Sent:	22nd May 20X5, 09.35am
Subject:	Marketing Strategy for 99

Morning Alex,

I am aware that rumours are already circulating around the company about a possible "take-over", and I want to address this by holding a conference this afternoon to provide accurate information and assure everybody that we will be continuing to operate our business as usual, whether the deal goes ahead or not. I have a meeting with Zero's management this morning where I can get some more information, but in the meantime I need you to help me by emailing your ideas to me on the following topics for my presentation:

- Explain the reasons why a strong brand is so important to companies such as 99.

- Describe the key aspects of the product and place mix involved in a deal between Zero and 99.

- Discuss the main strategic threats in marketing that 99 will face.

I will need this information by midday.

Many thanks,
Eric

Eric Winter
Managing Director, 99

Write your response to the email from Eric Winter

Task 29 - Factoring

(indicative timing : 30 minutes)

Phil's Pies was started as a cottage industry with Sue making homemade pies from her farmhouse kitchen, whilst her husband, Phil, worked the farm. The company has been growing rapidly over the last 5 years and now has its own factory. Sue would like to improve efficiency by buying a new automated pie baking machine. Phil's Pies employs 20 full time staff, 3 of these staff members work in the office with you and Sue, looking after the administrative tasks for the company.

Most of the regular customers order their pies each week. Last year Sue introduced credit terms, allowing customers to order on account and pay 30 days later. This increased both the number of new customers and also the amount ordered each week by existing customers. However, many customers are slow to pay and need to be regularly reminded by the office staff. Sue is considering the use of without recourse factoring to manage trade receivables. The factoring company will charge a fee of 2.5% of invoiced sales. It will give an advance of 90% of invoiced sales and charge interest at a rate of 12% per annum. Current credit terms are 30 days and this would not change with the factoring agreement. The company currently finances its accounts receivables with a bank overdraft at an interest rate of 15%per annum.

Today is 12th May 20X5

As the company accountant, you are concerned about the costs involved in engaging a factoring company and you recently prepared the following report detailing the financial costs and benefits of using the factoring company:

To: Sue Stackhouse
From: Jess Jones
Date of Report: 5th May 20X5

Calculation of the annual cost of factoring net of credit control cost savings.

		$
Factoring Fee based on revenue	$1,095,000 × 2.5%	27,375
Annual interest based on receivables	$180,000 × 90% × 12%	19,440
Total		46,815
Less saving on credit control costs		(20,000)
Total		26,815

Current Borrowings = $180,000 × 90% × 15% = $24,300

Therefore there is no financial benefit from using the factors at a cost of $26,815. It is cheaper to borrow using the bank overdraft.

Phil's Pies could improve credit control and reduce administration costs by preparing an aged analysis report each week. For example, an age analysis of trade receivables, for customer Carl's Cafe, at 30 April 20X5 showing the outstanding balance analysed by month:

Customer	Balance	Up to 30days	Up to 60 days	Up to 90 days	Over 90 days
Carl's Cafe	701	145	438	0	118

This morning, Sue sent you the following e-mail:

From: Sue Stackhouse SS@PhilsPies.co.uk
To: Jess Jones JJ@PhilsPies.co.uk
Sent: 12th May 20X5, 9.27am
Subject: Factoring

Dear Jess,

I have a meeting with our bank manager this afternoon to discuss either arranging a loan for the new $150,000 pie machine, or looking at a hire purchase agreement. In preparation, please could you send me an email by midday to clarify the following for me:

- Discuss two benefits to Phil's Pies of introducing the process of preparing an age analysis of trade receivables each week.

- Explain the non-financial benefits of the use of a factoring company.

- Compare and contrast medium term funding by means of a bank loan or hire purchase agreement.

Many thanks,
Sue

Sue Stackhouse
Managing Director, Phil's Pies

Write your response to the email from Sue Stackhouse

Task 30 - Greek

(indicative timing : 30 minutes)

Greek Ltd manufactures and sells a single product, the Alpha, and operates a standard absorption costing system. A predetermined absorption rate is used for fixed production overheads and is based on normal capacity of 20,000 units per month.

Nico Straton, the Managing Director, has just returned from a marketing conference where it was suggested that businesses should be using marginal costing rather than absorption costing for decision making and price setting. You were therefore asked to provide a reconciliation between the absorption costing profit and the marginal costing profit as part of the April period end management accounts (see Exhibit 1)

Exhibit 1: Extract from April management accounts

Reconciliation of the absorption costing profit for the month of April with the profit using marginal costing.

Closing inventory is 2000 units higher than opening inventory therefore absorption costing will show a higher profit than marginal costing. The Overhead absorption rate is currently $2.50 per unit.

Profit for April using absorption costing		$79,000
less (change in inventory level × OAR)	(2,000 × $2.50)	$(5,000)
Profit using marginal costing		$74,000

Greek Ltd is also considering introducing a new product, the Beta. Market research suggests that the selling price per unit should be $24, $25 or $26. The marketing department has produced estimates of sales demand and their associated probabilities for each possible selling price. These estimates are based on pessimistic, likely and optimistic forecasts (see Exhibit 2)

Exhibit 2: Marketing estimated sales demand and associated probabilities

Selling Price	$24		$25		$26	
	Sales Demand Units	Probability	Sales Demand Units	Probability	Sales Demand Units	Probability
Pessimistic	70,000	0.2	60,000	0.1	30,000	0.3
Likely	80,000	0.5	70,000	0.6	60,000	0.4
Optimistic	90,000	0.3	90,000	0.3	70,000	0.3

Today is 25th May 20X5

You have just received the following extract from the board meeting minutes from 20th May 20X5:

Greek Ltd

Meeting Minutes: 20th May 20X5
Next meeting: 19th June 20X5

Nico raised the subject of inventory valuation and wants Greek Ltd to investigate his proposal to move from absorption costing to marginal costing. He feels this will provide better information for new product pricing strategies.

The board also discussed the launch of a new product, the Beta. Market research suggests that the selling price per unit should be $24, $25 or $26. The marketing department has produced estimates of sales demand and their associated probabilities for each possible selling price. These estimates are based on pessimistic, likely and optimistic forecasts. This product has a different cost structure and is much more expensive to manufacture than the existing Alpha, so it is essential that the correct pricing strategy is determined before product launch.

Nico sends you the following e-mail:

From: Nico Straton NS@Greek.co.uk
To: Morgan Williams MW@Greek.co.uk
Sent: 25th May 20X5, 10.27am
Subject: Alpha and Beta

Dear Morgan,

Now that new product development are satisfied we have developed a product that can be manufactured consistently, and marketing have determined that there is an opportunity in the market for this product, we need to finalise the numbers so that we can move into manufacture and launch the Beta without further delay.

To help the board decision on costing and pricing, please could you provide us with further information on these techniques:

- Explain the advantages and disadvantages of the two costing approaches

- Discuss how helpful each costing approach is for price setting

- Describe problems that might arise with basing decisions on Expected Values (EV)

We have a product launch meeting this afternoon and I would like to be able to present this information there.

Many thanks,
Nico

Write your response to the email from Nico Straton

Topic 6 – E1 Primary Tasks Solutions

Task 25

Marking scheme

	Marks
Explaining HOW the ERP system could help LD2 Up to 1 mark for each relevant point	8
Explaining privacy and security issues Up to 1 mark for each relevant point	5
Explaining features of a corporate website Up to 1 mark for each relevant point	6
Recommend a changeover strategy for LD2 Up to 2mark for definitions of each changeover type Up to 4 marks for recommendation with justification	6 — 25

Our answer shows what we consider the most appropriate points to make. Other relevant points that answer the question would earn marks. However, irrelevant points that do not answer the question would not earn marks.

Suggested solution:

> From: Sarah Walker SW@LD2.co.uk
> To: Bob Carter BC@LD2.co.uk
> Sent: 12th May 20X5, 12.45am
> Subject: New ERP System
>
> Dear Bob,
>
> In response to your email this morning, I have answered each of your queries in turn below:
>
> 1.   **The ways in which the proposed ERP system will benefit LD2 include:**
>
> **Integration of systems.**
>
> The new system will provide one single system that replaces a number of separate systems. A single system will solve the current problems due to incompatibility of software between different systems, and remove the need for complex reconciliation of system output. This means that management information will be more accurate and finance can be freed up to support decision-making rather than verifying the figures. This should mean that Management Reports are provided on time going forward.

Cost and quality.

The new system should support a simpler and better quality of operation resulting in lower operating costs. Separate systems are more costly because they require different input and reconciliation of output. Currently a lot of errors are present in the data, reducing the quality and validity of decision made using it. This will in part be due to the manual nature of a lot of the data. The ERP system will automate much of this data generation, improving its reliability, accuracy and therefore quality. With an integrated system, data will be input just once, reducing input time, effort and cost. Staff are then freed up to support and improve the customer service and project management aspects of the business.

Inventory Management

With a shared system across all kitchen accessory, supply and fit operations it will be easier to identify products that can be shared across the operations to streamline products and reduce the number of inventory Stock Keeping Units (SKU). Holding levels of inventory can also be reduced by managing the inventory centrally and removing the buffer stock per operation. The current issues of stock shortages should be prevented by the more accurate and real-time reporting available. In particular, the manual nature of a lot of the company data means that management do not currently have view of much of the existing inventory held. Automation and integration of this data will more reliably inform management decisions such as the ability to identify and share stock across the operational units.

Fewer errors.

The new system should be designed to reduce the likelihood of undetected input and of input errors. The new system should enable management to submit accurate timesheet entries directly into a central payroll system, eliminating the faulty data input currently occurring. Calculations should be done within the system, by the software to eliminating the current issue of incorrectly calculated payroll and invoice values.

Capacity for growth.

The LD2 group has grown by acquiring other businesses, a strategy which may continue. The ERP system should be designed so that it can take on additional processing capacity that may be required in the future, for example allowing acquired businesses to be transferred to the system following acquisitions.

Comparative efficiency.

LD2's technology currently lags behind that of its competitors. A new system will enable LD2 to utilise current technology and incorporate the latest business best practice processes to, (hopefully) overtake the competition.

2. **The privacy and security issues that may need to be considered**

   Information security involves preventing unauthorised access, use, disclosure, disruption and destruction of information.

   There is a **legal duty** to maintain information securely under the Data Protection Act. There may also be a legal duty to keep certain data confidential – e.g. supplier agreements

   LD2 could suffer **reputational damage** if personal data of staff, or company data of customers and suppliers leaked.

   Company information such as product design, investment plans for the future, future pricing/marketing strategies or new product launches provide a **source of competitive advantage** which will be compromised by this information being leaked, and could have external impacts. For example if a takeover target was leaked, the share price would rise

3. **LD2's new corporate website should include the following features if it is to compare with the best in the industry:**

   Easily found.

   A corporate website should be easily located through the main search engines (eg Google) and should appear on the first page of the list of website addresses. The name of the website should also be easy to remember. This will give LD2 an advantage over its competition as potential customers find our website first. To encourage them to explore, the website should be designed in such a way that it is attractive and appealing to users.

   Providing information that users require.

   The website must contain all the information that users expect, so that when they visit the website they find what they are looking for. For example, our potential customers may find a kitchen design feature useful and attract them to come into store to view our product ranges. The information on the website should be continually refreshed and kept up-to-date to keep up with changing trends in consumer fashion.

   Easy to navigate.

   The website should be easy to navigate so users are able to find what they are looking for quickly and easily. For example, users may want to search by style of kitchen cabinet, or search based on colour. Information should not be 'buried' in the site, it should be available within a few clicks. The site should include a search facility to help with the location of information.

   E-commerce.

   The website should enable customers to buy the company's products or services. E-commerce is an important revenue stream for most businesses. Payment processing must be secure. This will enable supply-only customers to design their kitchen and purchase all require parts from their own home, extending the current market for LD2 to anywhere in the country. The website should also encourage feedback from these customers and provide a facility that allows them to ask questions or to make comments about the quality of the company's goods or services.

4. **Recommendation on most suitable change over method**

There are four main change over methods to be considered:

Direct changeover involves implementing a new IT system in full and at one time.

Phased changeover involves introducing parts of the new system in stages.

Parallel running involves operating the old and the new systems together for a short period of time

Pilot schemes involve introducing the new system in one or two selected areas or offices first.

Direct changeover is recommended for the following reasons:

Cost

A direct changeover will be less costly than any other method of implementing the new system, as only one set of system licensing and maintenance fees will be payable at any time. This choice will save money.

Acceptable risk

Usually direct changeover increases risk, but given that a lot of existing systems are manual or paper based, we could take the view that there are unlikely to be any operational problems with introducing the new system in full immediately. The risk of direct change could therefore be considered to be acceptable. Since the ERP system selected is an off-the-shelf software that has been used successfully in many other organisations, the risk can be considered to be very low.

I hope my explanations above provide the information you require. Please let me know if you require any further information.

Kind Regards,
Sarah

Sarah Walker
Management Accountant, LD2

Competency coverage

Sub-task	Technical		Business acumen		People		Leadership		Max
1	Knowledge of ERP	2	Advantages to be gained from an ERP system	6					8
2			Knowledge of the regulatory environment	2	Communicating privacy and security issues	3			5
3	Features of a corporate website	6							6
4	Knowledge of alternative change over strategies	4			Decision-making to recommend a change over strategy	2			6
Total		12		8		5			25

Sub-task 1 requires a demonstration of technical knowledge on ERP and recognition of strategic advantages of implementing ERP, effectively helping the Managing Director sell the benefits of the new ERP system to the rest of the Board and the company Shareholders. Sub-task 2 requires a demonstration of knowledge of the regulatory framework in the context of date security and using influencing skills to help the Managing Director to reassure the rest of the Board and the Shareholders that all relevant privacy and security issues have been considered and addressed. Sub-task 3 requires a demonstration of the importance of the features suggested for the new corporate website. Sub-task 4 requires a knowledge of alternative strategies to be considered in the project management framework and then a demonstration of decision-making skills to influence the Managing Director on the most appropriate change-over strategy. All of these sub-topics also require application of theoretical knowledge to the company, LD2, and to the specifics of the scenario provided.

Task 26

Marking scheme

	Marks
Explaining how 2JN can achieve TQM Up to 1 mark for each relevant point	7
Identifying issues and work groups for training Up to 1 mark for each relevant point	6
Discussing how quality will help reduce costs and increase revenue Up to 3 mark for each relevant point	6
Explaining how process design could improve competitive advantage Up to 1 mark for each relevant point	6
	25

Our answer shows what we consider the most appropriate points to make. Other relevant points that answer the question would earn marks. However, irrelevant points that do not answer the question would not earn marks.

Suggested solution:

From: Andy Barker AB@2JN.co.uk
To: Martin Warwick MW@2JN.co.uk
Sent: 7th May 20X5, 11.55am
Subject: TQM Requirements

Dear Martin,

In response to your email this morning, I have answered each of your queries in turn below:

1. **Requirements for achieving a Total Quality Management (TQM) approach within 2JN.**

   TQM is the continuous improvement in quality, productivity and effectiveness. Its objective is to ensure that the quality of products meets or exceeds customer expectations and to achieve this, employees at all levels of the organisation need to be involved.

   The requirements for 2JN to introduce TQM include:

   Leadership

   2JN's move towards TQM is currently being put forward by John. However, in order for the change to go through successfully, John needs to gain the acceptance and support of all of the senior members of the company. Presentations and briefings need to be provided to each member of the senior team to ensure they understand the benefits TQM will deliver to 2JN. The requirement of their department to attend training sessions and workshops to review current working practices will also need to be understood and accepted.

Internal suppliers and customers

Senior Management buy-in will ensure the various departments within 2JN view themselves as suppliers and customers of other departments within the organisation. This will lead to the development of quality chains as each part of the chain improves the quality for the next link (or customer) in the chain. It would be useful in your presentation to give an example to help the supervisors understand what this means. The operatives in the Assembly department are customers of the Goods inwards department. They can therefore expect to receive the right material, at the right quality and in the right quantity at the start of each shift. This will enable Assembly to do their jobs without stoppages due to short supply or machine blockages due to inferior quality sheet metal. Assembly are internal suppliers to the Paint Shop and must ensure the product has been fully assembled and meets the quality specification before it is transferred.

Commitment& Team Working

Employees throughout the organisation need to commit to building quality into everything they do. This commitment needs to come from staff sharing the quality philosophy rather than being coerced into the change. This will require a change in Performance measures from the current traditional manufacturing targets of units produced per shift and cost per employee. With the introduction of TQM a more appropriate measure would be number of rejects per shift and hours of training per employee per month.2JN should emphasise the importance of employees working as teams and assist in their development in the workplace.

Empowerment

For TQM to be successful, employees need to be empowered to make decisions without the need to refer to a supervisor or manager for approval. This will involve training to ensure each operative is confident in the skills they need to do their job, and that they understand the role they play in the organisation. They should also be encouraged and praised for raising quality issues as this provides 2JN with the opportunity to continue to improve operations. Supervisor's time is now freed up from telling staff what to do, and this enables more time to focus on value-added activities such as product design improvements and optimising process flow.

Relationships with suppliers

To achieve high quality output, 2JN needs to be able to rely on high quality inputs from its suppliers. This will require the forging of closer relationships with suppliers to enable the organisation to rely on the quality of its raw materials. If possible, suppliers should operate TQM as well. This means that purchasing need to move away from their traditional focus of driving cost savings by maximising the use bulk buy discounts. Instead, contracts should be negotiated to source and keep suppliers who consistently deliver the right material, of the right quality, in the right quantity and when it is needed. Finance play their part here as well. To keep these suppliers happy we need to ensure we pay them correctly and on time.

2.   **Issues and work groups that need to be considered when organising the TQM training in 2JN.**

Training

Introducing TQM means considerable training and support is required at all levels of the organisation. This will have a cost implication and productivity is likely to fall in the short-term as employees get to grips with the requirements of TQM.

Pat has already been tasked with arranging training ready for the introduction of TQM. She will need to consider a number of groups and issues.

Training strategy

As TQM will affect every part of the business it is important that 2JN develops an effective training strategy to ensure the training meets the needs of the business, all the objectives of TQM are met and all staff receive the necessary support. As I have already explained above, this is not just about the factory operative, but also includes a change in focus for the Supervisors and Purchasing staff, as well as improvements in invoice processing and payment by Finance.

Needs of individuals

TQM will affect employees in different parts of the business differently. Therefore the training provided to different groups within the organisation will need to be tailored to their specific roles. Your presentation to the factory supervisors this afternoon is the first step towards this. It may also be helpful to Pat to attend, and also shows her support for the programme. If the supervisors can understand the benefits to the company, they are more likely to work with Pat to identify the training requirements of their team and this should result in far less resistance to change across the factory operatives. Pat should spend some time learning about the organisation-wide impact of TQM and then hold briefing meetings with each department manager to provide a training programme tailored to the needs of each department.

Training provider

Pat should give careful thought into who provides the training. A project on this scale will require each Supervisor to manage the process of introducing TQM to their work production unit. It is likely that a provider with experience of introducing TQM into a manufacturing organisation would be the best choice to train the Supervisors. The Supervisors should then be in a position to train their own staff. This approach could also be used in other departments, with each manager receiving the relevant training from an external provider and then cascading this learning to their team. This approach ensures expert knowledge is gained during training, but keeps the cost down by not using the external provider to train all staff. Each departmental manager or supervisor will be able to tailor this knowledge to their department's role in the organisation to ensure all staff understand the impact to their own role.

Location and cost

Consideration should be given to where the training is to take place as this will have a cost implication. Costs will be reduced if the training is provided at 2JN rather than at a venue that needs to be hired. However, this cost saving may be offset by the disruption it may cause to on-going operations. It may be worth considering off-site training for the managers and supervisors, but using on-site meeting rooms for training the rest of 2JN's workforce.

Evaluation

After the training has been completed its success should be evaluated in terms of whether or not it has met the objectives set for it. In 2JN's case it will be whether TQM has been successfully introduced and individuals have a clear understanding of their role. Individuals or teams that are not performing as expected may need further training and support.

The different groups within 2JN should be considered as follows:

The workforce

The workforce currently has no knowledge of TQM or what it involves. If TQM is introduced without educating them as to why it is important and reassuring them about what it means for their jobs then this may cause resistance to the change. Therefore training should begin with presentations and talks to get the message across. There should be time allowed to answer any questions asked. Once employees understand the change, then more job specific training can begin.

Supervisors

Supervisors will be responsible for implementing TQM in their teams. Once they have a good grounding in the philosophy behind TQM it is important that the training they receive supports their role in implementing it. This is likely to include the development of new skills such as problem solving, communication and people management.

Senior managers

The senior managers should be the first to be trained as they will be responsible for the general implementation of TQM in the organisation. For the implementation to be successful they need to demonstrate commitment and leadership to push the plan forward. This is specialist training which might be best provided off-site, especially to keep the plans confidential before they are announced to the workforce and supervisors.

Quality committee

The quality committee will oversee the entire process of introducing TQM into 2JN. Rather than see one aspect of TQM, they will be involved in all aspects of it and therefore members of the committee need a thorough grounding in all areas. Due to the volume of training it is likely that it will need to be provided over a longer period of time than other groups and with a more formal structure of it so the group stays focussed.

3. **High quality 'will both put costs down and revenue up'.**

   Quality may affect costs as follows:

   - By building quality into production, 2JN's costs of production will rise, but this could be off-set by reduction in costs of rework and scrapping defective goods.

   - External quality costs will fall as will the cost of any warranty claims.

   - The costs of quality inspection will fall as all employees are responsible for quality.

Quality may affect revenue as follows:

- Revenue may increase as 2JN's reputation for quality improves and its products become more attractive to new customers.

- Sales may be increased by a reduction in prices driven by falling costs.

- 2JN should find it easier to retain customers once they realise quality is increasing. This should help stop the decline in profitability.

4. **Improve competitive performance through process design**

Process design

Process design involves analysing and seeking to understand the activities or processes that enable an organisation to function. The aim is to ensure that these activities or processes are designed so as to be as effective and efficient as possible. Process design can be applied to the development of new processes or (as with 2JN) it can be applied to improve existing processes. Two tools often used in the context of process design are **Business process reengineering** (BPR) and **process maps**.

The use of BPR

Business process reengineering (BPR) is the fundamental rethinking and radical redesign of business processes to achieve dramatic improvements in performance, such as cost, quality, service and speed.2JN could use BPR to redesign its processes with the aim of working more efficiently and streamlining the flow of operations to remove the non-value added transportation of goods around the factory and re-work created by damaging goods during this process. This will bring down costs of handling, rework and scrap. BPR could also play a part to help bring about improvements in **supply chain management**. BPR can be a **costly process**, so the benefits need to outweigh the cost of implementation and the ongoing cost of operating and working under the new processes.

The use of process maps

One way of analysing and representing processes is with the use of process maps. Process mapping aims to identify and represent the steps involved in a process, in visual form. The use of process maps will help 2JN design effective and efficient operations by helping establish how efficient the process is and **identify any waste.** In particular any duplication of tasks across work production units can be eliminated.

Changing systems and working methods (for example, via BPR) without understanding the underlying processes can lead to costly mistakes. It can also create conditions that make it difficult for staff to work effectively. Moreover, if 2JN does not understand a process, it will not be able to improve it. Process mapping will enable 2JN to **clearly define and understand current processes**. It will help identify likely problem areas such as bottlenecks, delays or waste. The knowledge that process mapping provides will help 2JN to **develop solutions** and plan new, improved processes. These can then also be used by Pat as part of the training documentation to help explain the change in each process.

Improving 2JN's competitive performance

Management of the supply chain and supply network is now seen as a potential source of **competitive advantage**. By adopting a more strategic approach to supply chain management, 2JN can improve its competitive performance through greater **coordination** across the global supply network. This means that Supervisors will start to work more closely with purchasing and sales to ensure the products produced are of the expected quality for our customers.

Key considerations would be:

- **Partnering with other companies** in the supply network (organisational integration) by reducing the number of suppliers used, so deeper relationships can be developed with a select few (perhaps selected using cost-benefit analysis).Reliability, trust and collaboration is highly important.

- Restructuring the organisation to better facilitate closer supplier relationships and control processes should improve 2JN's ability to meet **demanding customer service and product performance standards**. Innovation in consumer goods is required if products are to remain attractive to consumers.

- Establishing a **supply chain network by** interconnecting with key suppliers through linkages between the different processes and activities involved in producing products/services.

- **Outsource non-core activities**, such as the distribution. The benchmarking exercise you commissioned may have indicated that 2JN's competitors are already doing so, and that 2JN needs to catch up.

- Efficiencies can also be attained by **applying technology** to dealings with suppliers, using electronic data interchange (EDI) – this 'paperless' communication is more efficient in terms of administration, and is quicker and cheaper than traditional ordering methods.

I hope my explanations above provide the information you require. Please let me know if you require any further information.

Kind Regards,
Andy

Andy Barker
Management Accountant, 2JN

Competency coverage

Sub-task	Technical		Business acumen		People		Leadership		Max
1	Knowledge of TQM	5					Coaching & change management support for TQM	2	7
2			Change management for TQM implementation	4	Recognising collaborative necessity of working groups	2			6
3			Identifying advantage to be gained from quality approach	2	Collaborative working in TQM	4			6
4	Knowledge of BPR and Process maps	6							6
Total		11		6		6		2	25

Sub-task 1 requires a knowledge of TQM and a demonstration of business partnering skills to coach the Operations Director in TQM techniques and principles. Sub-task 2 requires a recognition of the need for working groups as part of the change management process and a recognition of the strategic importance of the successful implementation of a project. Sub-task 3 requires identification of the competitive advantage for companies taking a quality approach, as well as a demonstration of skills required to work collaboratively across teams. Sub-task 4 requires knowledge of BPR and Process maps. All of these sub-topics also require application of theoretical knowledge to the company, 2JN, and to the specifics of the scenario provided.

Task 27

Marking scheme

	Marks
Explaining ways teams can operate when geographically dispersed Up to 1 mark for each relevant point	7
Describing advantages and disadvantages of homeworking Up to 1 mark for each relevant point	8
Describing the role of HR in relation to homeworking Up to 1 mark for each relevant point	10
	25

Our answer shows what we consider the most appropriate points to make. Other relevant points that answer the question would earn marks. However, irrelevant points that do not answer the question would not earn marks.

Suggested solution:

> From: Sally Cooper SC@TB.co.uk
> To: Felicity Fox FF@TB.co.uk
> Sent: 1st May 20X5, 10.08am
> Subject: Home Working Proposal
>
> Dear Felicity,
>
> As requested, some explanations of the key points you may want to cover during your presentation to HR this afternoon are provided below:
>
> 1. **Challenges of managing geographically dispersed teams**
>
>   There are a number of ways in which managers of teams in companies like TB, that have team members spread across the world, can meet the challenges this brings.
>
>   **Use of technology to communicate and to tie the team together**
>
>   Team members spread around the world often find it difficult to visualise and identify with the wider team they are part of. TB is already utilising technology to improve communication. It could extend this to the use of shared resources held on a central server, for example an intranet. Communication is key to managing any team as it allows information to flow and for relationships to be built. Geographically dispersed teams are no different – it is just the type of communication which is different (being more often electronic rather than face-to-face).The team manager must be creative in their use of technology and willingness to use it. They should identify the types of communication which work best for their team and use them wherever possible. For sales and purchasing teams, this will involve regional team meetings in North, South, East and West, as well as Functional meetings involving staff across all locations. Some managers may find setting up a team page on a social media site helps build team spirit even though team members do not work together in the same office.

Consistent induction and training processes

It is important that all team members work in a similar way and all have the same understanding and knowledge. This can be difficult to achieve with team members based in different locations. A single, consistent induction and training programme can help ensure a consistent level of expectation, knowledge and performance across the whole team. This is something that HR would need to develop in conjunction with managers of virtual teams to understand the challenges that need to be addressed. In particular, homeworkers can feel quite isolated and need to know there is support available to ensure they can perform their role to the best of their ability. Again, a team page on a social media site could help provide support for the new members of the team from the longer serving team members. This will also help reduce some of the manager's time spent providing general TB guidance.

Clear lines of authority and role responsibility

A person's authority and responsibility is often communicated in part by their personality and 'in person' interactions with others. With geographically dispersed teams, relying upon electronic communication, these clues and informal discussions to establish responsibility are often absent. It is essential therefore that all team members are aware of the team structure, roles and responsibilities – these must be clear and available for all to see. For example, in global organisations, it is essential people know who is responsible for a particular customer or contract that operates in different regions. This information should all be easily accessible via TB's intranet.

Be aware of possible cultural differences

Employees who live in different locations and cultures may have different personal goals. For example, some cultures are more work focussed than others, with the achievement of promotion and status a key motivator. A manager of a geographically dispersed team should be aware of differences between goals of individuals within their team and to try to ensure all act in a way that helps achieve the organisation's goals. This may require devoting more time managing and mentoring employees than if they were in one central location.

Build team spirit

Building a sense of team spirit and cooperation can be more difficult when team members are spread around the world. Employees who only communicate by email or other electronic means do not share the spirit of collaboration to the same degree and communications become more pressured in tone and demands. For example an employee may only hear from another when their work is late or something has gone wrong. A manager of a dispersed team should encourage collaboration between employees. This may be achieved through face-to-face team building events but could also be achieved through giving employees projects to achieve as a team.

2.   Advantages and disadvantages of Homeworking

Homeworking involves staff performing their role at home and is made possible by developments in information technology. There are a number of advantages and disadvantages of this practice for TB's staff. These include:

Advantages of homeworking

Cost saving

Working at home saves the employee from having to pay expensive commuting costs such as petrol, car parking and train fares as well as lower value costs such as having suits dry cleaned and eating out at lunchtime.

Time saving

The elimination of commuting to the workplace also saves the employee valuable time at the start and end of the day, freeing time up for social pursuits and family time. However, this is being limited by TB as we are requiring them to work 50% of the time saving they would have had by no longer needing to commute.

Work/life balance

By working at home the employee is better positioned to balance their work and family commitments. For example they can fit doctors' appointments in during the day, collect children from school or perform voluntary work which would not be possible if they had to commute to their place of work.

Productivity

Employees often find they are more productive if they work from home as they can avoid interruptions that occur in the office as well as the benefits from being more relaxed in their own home. TB has estimated that staff who homework are 20% more productive.

Housing choice

Employees who do not commute have greater freedom when choosing a place to live. This means they can locate themselves in places where they can afford to buy a house or pay rent or that are more suitable for their family and lifestyle.

Disadvantages of homeworking

Loss of space

The employee needs to create an office space to work in and for any necessary IT equipment. This may mean the loss of a whole room (often a bedroom) which must be sacrificed in order for them to work at home.

Increased utility bills

Certain bills, such as gas, electricity and water, may increase as a consequence of the employee being at home rather than in a traditional workplace.

Loss of social contact

Some employees thrive on the social contact that they receive at work. Colleagues often become friends and socialise away from work. Such opportunities would be reduced if a workforce works at home.

Use of home as an office

Employees may prefer to separate home life from work life. Bringing their work home means they are notable to make such a distinction and may find it difficult to 'switch off' after the working day is over.

Becoming distracted

Working away from the eye of a manager or supervisor may create a temptation for the employee to stop work and, for example, watch TV or play computer games. This may result in them becoming less productive and the quality of their work may suffer.

3. The role of HR in supporting homeworking

There are a number of **important roles** that **TB's HR department** can play given its working practices. These include:

Involving employees in the corporate culture New employees should be introduced to TB's corporate culture as part of their induction process. This is particularly important as employees are based in different countries and some may work mainly from home. The induction may be only one of a few opportunities for such employees to feel part of a wider 'family' and develop a shared vision of where the organisation is going.

Dealing with personnel issues arising from homeworking

The use of home working opens up a number of issues in which the HR department should become involved as and when necessary. This may include, for example, health and safety issues around employees home workstation, disciplinary action where employees are found not to be working or where the IT and telecoms equipment they are provided with is abused.

Ensuring comparability of remuneration

Salary levels between employees in different countries should be comparable (but at the same time competitive locally) - TB's HR department should be involved in ensuring that employees are neither over nor under paid for their role. This comparability should take into account the economy and overall pay levels within the country that the employee lives.

Legal compliance

TB's HR department should ensure TB meets all relevant employment law and regulations (such as health and safety rules) which affect it and its employees around the world. This will minimise the risk of TB being taken to court by employees or others for breaches of legislation (for example minimum notice periods which must be respected when an employee is dismissed).

Developing an appropriate appraisal system

It is the role of any HR department to develop an appraisal system which is appropriate to the businesses' needs. In a geographically dispersed organisation such as TB, this is complicated by the different cultures and working practices in which its employees work under. This means that it is also necessary to develop a sensible system of recording and comparing employee performance. It should also make decisions on how best to allocate bonuses or other performance related remuneration.

I hope my explanations above provide the information you require. Please let me know if you require any further information.

Kind Regards,
Sally

Sally Cooper
Management Accountant, TB

Competency coverage

Sub-task	Technical		Business acumen		People		Leadership		Max
1					Collaborative working	7			7
2			homeworking	8					8
3	HR role working practices	10						10	10
Total		10		8		7		10	25

Sub-task 1 requires a demonstration of knowledge of virtual team logistics and an understanding of how to maintain a collaborative working environment. Sub-task 2 requires an understanding of the competitive advantages to be gained from employing home workers. Sub-task 3 requires a demonstration of knowledge of HR practices relating to home working. All of these sub-topics also require application of theoretical knowledge to the company, TB, and to the specifics of the scenario provided.

Task 28

Marking scheme

	Marks
Explaining the importance of a strong brand Up to 1 mark for each relevant point	7
Describing aspects of product mix and place mix between Zero and 99 Up to 1 mark for each relevant point	8
Discussing the strategic threats 99 may face Up to 3 mark for each relevant point	10
	<u>25</u>

Our answer shows what we consider the most appropriate points to make. Other relevant points that answer the question would earn marks. However, irrelevant points that do not answer the question would not earn marks.

Suggested solution:

From: Alex Summer AS@99.co.uk
To: Eric Winter EW@99.co.uk
Sent: 22ndMay 20X5, 11.45am
Subject: Marketing Strategy for 99

Dear Eric,

Further to your email this morning, please see below for the main points I recommend you to include in your presentation this afternoon:

1.   **A strong brand is important to 99 for a number of reasons.**

A brand is an **aspect of 'product' in the marketing mix**, particularly for consumer products. A strong brand **helps to create the image of the product that the manufacturer want to present to the public**. In the case of manufacturers of environmentally-friendly products, such as 99, the brand name can help to deliver a message of the company's concern for the environment and the contribution of its products to protecting it.

99 could also use this brand, through advertising, to deliver a message that the company is contributing to providing cleaner water in poor communities around the world. Branding also helps a company to **differentiate its products** from those of its competitors. There are many producers of bottled water, but not so many that work to improve water quality in economically poor countries. The 99 brand may therefore help consumers to identify the company's products with **high ethical and moral standards**.

By purchasing the company's products, **consumers can feel that they are making a statement** of their concern for the environment, and help them to feel better about themselves. This will strengthen loyalty to the brand. As consumers become more environmentally-conscious, a brand name that consumers associate with concern for the environment should **help the company to sell more of its products**.

A strong brand may help a company such as 99 to ask for **premium prices** for its products, by making customers feel that they are buying something of better quality or value than when they buy a rival product. Even if the brand does not command premium prices (since there are many branded water products), it will nevertheless help customers to recognise the brand, so that **stockists are more willing to sell the company's products** and customers are more willing to buy them.

The ability of a company such as 99 to sell more products and at higher prices can be **financially significant**. Small companies may have high fixed costs relative to income, and although 99 pays its staff low wages or salaries, it will incur high costs of energy (since green energy is expensive) and probably also for distribution.

Brand names can help to **build customer loyalty** to a company's products. Once customers have started to buy a company's branded products, loyalty will make them buy the same brand the next time the make a purchase, in preference to other products on the shelves.

Successful brands are **intangible assets that have a value**. Companies such as 99 are likely to be taken over eventually by another larger company. Zero for example wants to acquire 99. A strong brand will enable the company to command a higher price from a buyer.

In summary, without a strong brand, small environmentally-conscious companies such as 99 may struggle to sell their products and operate profitably. With a strong brand, 99 can create a perception of a superior product that does good for society and the environment, so that some customers will be willing to pay a higher price.

2.   **Aspects of product mix and place mix in a deal between Zero and 99**

There are benefits for both 99 and Zero in a deal that has the potential to improve the product mix and place mix for both of them.

Product mix

The deal with Zero would enable 99 to make use of Zero's expertise to develop the 99 brand further. This may involve adding to 99's product range, expanding its product mix. A deal with Zero may involve further investment in the 99 brand name. The brand is an aspect of product, and a stronger brand would benefit the product mix for 99.

99 currently sells its products in ordinary plastic bottles, whereas Zero has plans to make all packaging biodegradable or recyclable. This form of packaging would strengthen the concept of 99's products as environmentally-friendly and so would strengthen its product mix. Zero has carbon labelling for its products. 99 may not have the facilities to do this, and a deal with Zero may therefore enable it to apply carbon labelling to its products for the first time. If so, this may add to the environmental 'credentials' of its products.

Zero may be willing to invest in improvements to operations at 99, so that 99 is able to offer its twoproducts in a wider variety of forms, such as in larger or smaller-sized bottles, or even with some form ofdiscrete flavouring. Adding to 99's product range would add to its product mix.For Zero, the acquisition of 99 would complement its product portfolio. This suggests that Zero does not yet sellbottled water. In principle, a large company could develop new products internally, but this would take time. The acquisition of 99 would enable it to obtain these new products immediately.

Place mix

At the moment 99 sells its products in a few garages, on airplane flights and in airport shops. Its distribution is therefore limited. 99 is currently unable to get its products stocked in supermarkets. A deal with Zero would enable 99 to sell through supermarkets, which would improve the place mix for 99.

Zero's distribution involves the use of low-carbon vehicles. It's likely that a deal with Zero would therefore make distribution more environmentally-friendly for 99's products. This would enable supermarkets to be supplied in an acceptable way to 99's customers, improving the place mix.99 could also make use of the entire distribution system of Zero, including its warehouses and inventory management systems as well as its distribution system.

An attraction of this deal is that Zero has promised to increase the number of water pumps supplied to poorer communities. This is indirectly related to place mix for 99, because the effect of the deal would be to increase the distribution of water pumps to communities around the world. For Zero, a deal with 99 would not affect its place mix significantly, except that its distribution systems would need to handle 99's products.

3. ### Strategic threats facing 99

    Strategic threats in marketing need to be identified as part of the strategic planning process. Marketing threats are external environmental factors that could prevent 99 from achieving our marketing goals. There are a number of forms these threats could take, from the emergence of new competitors or low-cost competitors to changing customer needs or regulatory changes that increase cost or make it difficult to comply. 99 could also face the impact of changes in the political, economic, social or technological environment.

    Political - New environmentally friendly governments could force the use of biodegradable materials. This would cause 99 to make the changes whether it wanted to or not. This would make the deal with Zero more attractive.

    Economic – if there is a recession, there may be a downturn in trade due to people's disposable incomes being reducing, and therefore they may spend less on bottled water.

    Social –if people in 99's country would rather see the money spent within the country helping the poor there, rather than overseas, this may lead them to spend their money with a competitor if that company helps local people instead.

    Technology – cheaper/more effective equipment becoming available would mean lower barriers to entry into the market and increased competition

These threats need to be continuously **monitored** and 99's marketing strategy adjusted as threats emerge. The activities of existing and emerging competitors can be monitored by use of the internet. Price comparison sites, for example, can alert us to low price competition.

The recently published national survey that highlighted a rising consumer demand for more environmentally and socially friendly products is likely to generate interest in the market from **new competitors**. This could threaten to reduce 99's market share. 99 needs to develop a customer loyalty strategy to protect the existing customer base or increase the barriers to entry for competitors. 99 should consider introducing a customer loyalty program that rewards customers for maintaining or increasing levels of business. Alternatively, forming strategic alliances with suppliers of essential components, such as the biodegradable packaging, will restrict access for competitors and create barriers to entry.

Weaknesses in the product and service portfolio, skills, distributor network or supply chain can increase vulnerability and make it difficult to respond to external threats. 99 needs to identify any weaknesses and prioritise actions to deal with the factors that represent greatest risk. This analysis can then be used to develop investment, recruitment or training strategies to overcome the problems. The acquisition by Zero will secure a "green" distribution network and help strengthen the service portfolio. 99 helps strengthen the product portfolio of Zero and so the acquisition would seem to benefit both companies.

I hope my explanations above provide the information you require. Please let me know if you require any further information.

Kind Regards,
Alex

Alex Summer
Accountant, 99

Competency coverage

Sub-task	Technical		Business acumen		People		Leadership		Max
1	Brand awareness	7							7
2					Product mix and Place mix	6	Product mix and Place mix	2	8
3	PEST model	4	PEST – Strategic threats in marketing	6					10
Total		11		6		6		2	25

Sub-task 1 requires a demonstration of understanding the importance of a strong brand image. Sub-task 2 requires a demonstration of the skills to drive performance through influencing the Product mix and Place mix. Sub-task 3 requires an analysis of the strategic threats and an awareness of the regulatory environment. All of these sub-topics also require application of theoretical knowledge to the company, 99, and to the specifics of the scenario provided.

Task 29

Marking scheme

	Marks
Discussing the benefits of an aged analysis report	
Up to 3 mark for each relevant point	6
Explaining non-financial benefits of factoring	
Up to 1 mark for each relevant point	5
Compare and contrasting bank loans and hire purchase agreements	
Up to 3 mark for each relevant point	6
	17

Our answer shows what we consider the most appropriate points to make. Other relevant points that answer the question would earn marks. However, irrelevant points that do not answer the question would not earn marks.

Suggested solution:

From: Jess Jones JJ@PhilsPies.co.uk
To: Sue Stackhouse SS@PhilsPies.co.uk
Sent: 12th May 20X5, 11.45am
Subject: Factoring

Dear Sue,

Further to your email this morning, please see below for the main points I recommend you consider before your bank meeting this afternoon:

1. **Two benefits to Phil's Pies of introducing the process of preparing an age analysis of trade receivables each week.**

   ### Decision-making

   The age analysis of receivables may be used to help decide what action to take about older debts. Old debts could be investigated, chased up or written off. If there is a persistent problem, Phil's Pies might have to insist on a refusal of credit. The Aged analysis illustrates whether there is a persistent problem with the customer, or a specific issues that needs to be resolved.

   For example, with Carl's Café most invoices are settled within 60 days. Phil's Pies have a credit term of 30 days, so we need to discuss this with Carl's Café to bring most payments within terms However, they are a good customer and pay regularly.

   There does however seem to be an issue with a small amount over 90 days and this suggests that there is a specific issue here. Phil's Pies needs to contact Carl's Café to understand why this invoice is not being paid and rectify the issue as soon as possible. It may be that we short delivered and a small credit is due from us to gain the remainder of the payment.

Control and targets

The age analysis can be used to monitor the efficiency of the cash collection and to ensure that collection is kept under control. Cash collection targets could be set for the office team to work to, and these reports would help ensure that these targets are met. I have already explained that Carl's Café pay within 60 days, yet their terms are 30 days. The aged analysis report highlights this and by producing the report weekly, the office team will be able to follow up on non-payment much faster to ensure better compliance to terms and better cash flow for Phil's Pies.

2.   **Non-financial benefits of the use of a factoring company.**

Speed – The Factoring company have agreed to advance 90% of the invoice value, and this is likely to be received within 24 hours, helping to maintain a good working cash flow rather than Phil's Pies waiting 30 days for a customer to pay. As with Carl's Café, we have seen that customers may not currently be paying on time.

This would be particularly useful if we received a large customer order that requires Phil's Pies to spend on stock and production costs before we get paid by the customer; factoring would allow Phil's Pies to accept the order with much less risk to our cash flow.

Time Saving – Factoring usually means the invoice finance company will collect the money themselves; saving Phil's Pies time and effort that we can use to benefit the business in other areas. For example, the 3 members of office staff could focus on customer service, or telephoning existing customers to prompt and increase regular orders.

Security – Factoring is secured on the sales already made and therefore would not require you to risk your home or business assets as security on the finance.

Funding Matches Your Business – As the business continues to grow and sales continue to increase, the amount of funding available through factoring is automatically increased because it will always be 90% of the current invoiced sales. Having funding that expands as you grow is extremely useful; particularly as many businesses fail because expanding sales use up their cash flow. This could be useful for funding the new pie machine.

Suitable for Businesses of All Sizes - One big advantage of factoring is that it is potentially suitable for businesses of all sizes; especially now there are invoice finance firms that are targeted at small businesses and their needs.

3.   **Bank loan versus hire purchase agreement.**

Term Loan

Phil's Pies will take out a loan for a lump sum in return for agreeing to make regular repayments. Fixed or variable interest is charged on the amount borrowed. There is usually a requirement for security in the form of an asset. If Phil's Pies had no assets, then as the business owner you may choose to use a personal asset such as your home. This can be very risky, because if the business does not make sufficient money to make the loan payments as they become due, then the bank can seize the asset and sell it to cover the cost of the loan. In this instance, the loan would be for the Pie Machine, so the bank may be prepared to provide a loan against the value of the pie machine if we can prove that the machine will maintain its value, at least in the short term.

Hire Purchase

Under a hire purchase agreement we would technically be hiring the pie machine and Phil's Pies would therefore not own the asset until it had been pay for in full.

One advantage over a term loan is that a Hire Purchase agreement often allows for some of the loan repayment to be deferred until the end of the agreement. Deferring part of the purchase price until the end of the agreement means more interest would be paid when compared to the bank loan, but would improve cash flow during the period of hire purchase.

At the end of the loan agreement, Phil's Pies could either pay the outstanding amount and take full ownership of the pie machine or sell the pie machine and use the money to pay off the deferred amount.

I hope my explanations above provide the information you require. Please let me know if you require any further information.

Kind Regards,
Jess

Jess Jones
Management Accountant, Phil's Pies

Competency coverage

Sub-task	Technical		Business acumen		People		Leadership		Max
1	Advantages of aged analysis	4			Communication elements of aged analysis	2			6
2	Non-financial benefits of factoring	3					Non-financial benefits of factoring	2	5
3	Bank Loan versus Hire Purchase	3	Bank Loan versus Hire Purchase	3					6
Total		10		3		2		2	17

Sub-task 1 requires a recognition of the importance of routine management reporting and its use in communicating across the business. Sub-task 2 knowledge of non-financial benefits of factoring and how it can be used to enhance business performance . Sub-task 3 requires knowledge of bank loans and hire purchase agreements. All of these sub-topics also require application of theoretical knowledge to the company, Factoring, and to the specifics of the scenario provided.

Task 30

Marking scheme

	Marks
Explaining the advantages and disadvantages Up to 1 mark for each relevant point	6
Discussing the costing method used for price setting Up to 3 mark for each relevant point	8
Describing problems with basing decisions on Expected Values Up to 1 mark for each relevant point	3
	17

Our answer shows what we consider the most appropriate points to make. Other relevant points that answer the question would earn marks. However, irrelevant points that do not answer the question would not earn marks.

Suggested solution:

From: Morgan Williams MW@Greek.co.uk
To: Nico Straton NS@Greek.co.uk
Sent: 25th May 20X5, 12.45am
Subject: Alpha and Beta

Dear Nico,

1.   **Advantages/disadvantages of the two costing approaches**

Advantages of Absorption Costing

At the end of March, and again at the end of April, Greek Ltd produced more Alpha than we sold. This means that Greek Ltd had finished goods in inventory. Using absorption costing has an advantage when some product remains unsold at the end of the period. In absorption costing, the fixed costs are assigned using a per-unit amount, and therefore each product in inventory has a value that includes part of the fixed overhead. This means that we do not show the expense until the item is sold. This can improve profits for the period.

Disadvantages of Absorption Costing

However, this means that the profit-and-loss statement does not show the full expenses incurred in the period if more goods remain unsold at the end of the period that at the start of the period. This can artificially inflate the profit figures in any given accounting period, which can be misleading when analysing profitability. The figures for April showed a higher profit for the period under absorption costing than we would achieve if we used marginal costing.

Advantages of Marginal Costing

Marginal costing shows profits after all the bills have been paid for the accounting period. When some product manufactured in the period is not sold in that period, the revenue has not yet been received, but the company has had to pay all expenses incurred in manufacturing the product. So marginal costing accounts for all expenses even though some revenue is still to be received. This means that when the product is eventually sold, the company has surplus income.

Disadvantages of Marginal Costing

As we saw in April, the process of marginal costing means that less profit is shown for the period because the complete overhead expense is shown even when there are still unsold products. This means that the company shows a reduced income because of unsold products but still shows the full expenses for overhead.

2. **How helpful it is for price setting**

Advantages of marginal pricing

Marginal costing is good for short-term decision-making because it focuses on recovering the variable costs of production and therefore recovering the additional cost to the company of manufacturing one unit of Beta. This is useful because Alpha is already making a sufficient profit to pay for all of the fixed overheads. By setting a marginal cost-plus price there is the potential to price lower than the competition.

Marginal costing also avoids having to make an arbitrary allocation of fixed costs and overheads. Currently we only produce one product, so it is reasonable to allocate the overhead cost equally to all products. However, once we launch the Beta, Greek will produce two products with very different cost bases and potentially manufacturing requirements. This will lead to the arbitrary allocation of overheads being less accurate and reliable.

Focuses the business on what is required to achieve break-even. In particular at product launch, Greek needs to gain and maintain as much market share as possible before the competition develop a similar product. It is therefore useful to understand the lowest price we could set for the product without causing the company to make a loss.

Disadvantages of marginal pricing

There is a risk that the price set will not recover total fixed costs in the long term. As long as Greek continues to sell Alpha at its current price this should not be an issue. Ultimately businesses must price their products in a way that reflects the total costs of the business. It may also be difficult to raise prices if the contribution per unit is set too low initially since customers will be used to this low product price and any increase in price could lead customers to seek out substitutes.

Advantages of absorption pricing

Greek already uses absorption costing, so there would be no change to current processes. It is also quite easy to derive a product price using this method, since it is based on a simple formula that does not have to be calculated by someone with specialised training.

In addition, as long as the budget assumptions used to derive the price turn out to be correct and a profit margin is added, a company will probably earn a profit if it uses this method to calculate prices.

Disadvantages of absorption pricing

This method ignores competition and the need for a competitive price. Greek could set the product price of Beta based on the absorption pricing formula and then find that competitors are charging substantially different prices.

The Beta could be priced too high or too low in comparison to what buyers are willing to pay. Thus, Greek either ends up pricing too low and giving away potential profits, or pricing too high and achieving minor revenues.

Additionally, the pricing formula is based on budget estimates of costs and sales volume, both of which may be incorrect.

Evaluation of absorption pricing

Ultimately, this method is not acceptable for deriving the price of a product that is to be sold in a competitive market, because it does not account for the pricing of competitors, nor does it factor in the value of the product to customers. A more realistic approach is to price each of products Alpha and Beta at the market price, so that both products, with varying profit margins, can absorb all expenses incurred by the company. Market research has confirmed that a price of $24-$26 would be acceptable to customers, so this is the target range of prices to aim for. It may be best simply to use this approach to compare absorption-based prices to market prices, to see if a company's cost structure will allow it to turn a profit.

3. **Problems with basing decisions on Expected Values**

The probabilities used are usually very subjective. In the case of Beta, the marketing department have estimated these probabilities, but they have not provided information on how they have determined these estimate. The only other product that Greek makes and sells is the Alpha. This is a very different product, with a different cost structure and therefore sales patterns may not be indicative of what we are likely to see for the Beta.

The EV is merely a weighted average and therefore has little meaning for a one-off project. Although the sales demand will be repeated annually, it is likely that external factors such as new regulations or new competition would impact the demand and expected selling price.

The EV gives no indication of the dispersion of possible outcomes about the EV, i.e. the risk. Again, there are a number of external factors that could impact the likely sales demand, and this will be linked to the product price, both at launch and throughout the product life-cylce.

I hope my explanations above provide the information you require. Please let me know if you require any further information.

Kind Regards,
Morgan

Morgan Williams
Management Accountant, Greek Ltd

Competency coverage

Sub-task	Technical		Business acumen		People		Leadership		Max
1	Advantages and disadvantages of Absorption costing and Marginal Costing	4					Advantages and disadvantages of Absorption costing and Marginal Costing	2	6
2			Relevance of each costing approach for price setting	4	Relevance of each costing approach for price setting	4			8
3	Disadvantages of Expected Value for business decisions	3							3
Total		7		4		4		2	17

Sub-task 1 requires knowledge of absorption costing and marginal costing, and a demonstration of the usefulness of different costing methods for driving elements of performance . Sub-task 2 requires a recognition of the strategic importance in selecting the right costing method to drive decisions on price setting. Sub-task 3 requires knowledge of the expected value technique. All of these sub-topics also require application of theoretical knowledge to the company, Factoring, and to the specifics of the scenario provided.

Topic 6 – E1 Further Tasks

Task 31 - S&C

(indicative timing : 45 mins)

You are Miranda Mills, a management accountant at S & C, a medium-sized consultancy firm that is experiencing rapid growth evidenced by increased turnover. It has been able to develop a range of new specialist business advisory services that it offers to its growing customer base.

The existing operational systems are struggling to cope with these new services, but a replacement system that includes state-of-the-art software is due to be installed within the next six months. The new system was justified because it could reduce costs and subsequently improve productivity, although precise details have not been given.

Due to the nature of S&C's business, no software will fit exactly with its processes. However, the replacement system has the clear advantage of giving S & C access to a state-of-the-art system which is not yet available to its competitors.

As well as the users of the system, other groups within S & C that have an interest in it are managers of the users and the senior management team.

Today is 7th May 20X5

A meeting of the firm's project steering group was held. Extracts from the minutes of the meeting include:

Minutes

It was decided that a phased approach should be used to introduce the new system.

The system will mostly be used by users who will enter data and write reports.

The managers of the users will be responsible for administering the system and for its security.

The reports written by the users will be sent to the Senior Managers who will review the work.

A programme of events for implementing the system has been agreed but is not yet fully operational.

It is not clear how to resolve the issue of poor strategic fit between the new system and the operational requirements of the organisation.

Senior managers should meet to discuss implementation issues.

You receive the following e-mail from Paul Perker, your line manager and a senior member of staff at S&C.

From: Paul Perker PP@SandC.co.uk
To: Miranda Mills MM@SandC.co.uk
Sent: 7th May 20X5, 10.15am
Subject: System implementation

Miranda,

A senior managers' meeting is due to take place tomorrow and I need your help to prepare a presentation on implementation issues regarding the new system.

As you are no doubt aware, the senior management team are conscious that system implementation represents a form of organisational change and they would like to be briefed about the approach that will be taken to the introduction of the new system and on likely changes to working practices, critical areas for success, system testing, support after implementation, system effectiveness, etc.

Please could you prepare some briefing notes on the following areas:

- The importance of ensuring the system is aligned with the firm's business strategy, including the options to overcome the fact that the software does not fit existing business processes exactly.

- Why a phased approach to introducing the system is, in this case, more suitable than a direct 'big bang' approach.

- How users should be involved in the implementation phase of the project.

- The training that should be given to the users, managers and senior managers.

- How the success or failure of the system could be evaluated.

Many thanks,

Paul

Paul Perker
Senior Manager, S&C
E: PP@SandC.co.uk
T: 0208 300 4000

Write your response to the email from Paul Perker

Task 32 - YO and MX

(indicative timing : 45 mins)

You are Colin Radner, a management account at YO. YO employs buyers, designers, machinists, tailors and sales people to produce and sell its coats, jackets, trousers, dresses and skirts.

YO has a long standing relationship with MX which sells directly to the public from a chain of out of town stores. Over 80% of YO's sales are to MX whose approach has been to sell clothing in great volumes at lower prices than the high street stores. MX expects its suppliers (including YO) to take account of new fashion designs and to manufacture its clothes at competitive prices.

MX is rethinking its strategy and wishes to move more 'upmarket' by introducing a better quality clothing range, which it believes its customers will be prepared to pay a little more for. Already YO has noticed that MX has started to be more demanding by sending back any batches of clothes it feels are in the slightest way unsuitable.

The following is an extract from the minutes of a recent meeting between the directors of YO and MX.

The directors of MX made the following points:

(1) MX wants to work with fewer suppliers, but to develop a better relationship with each of them.

(2) MX has stated that it wants to renegotiate its contract with YO (which expires soon in any case).

(3) MX is prepared to talk with YO about the need to improve the quality of its products and MX has indicated that if it receives the right assurances, it would be prepared to pay a slightly higher unit price per item.

(4) MX proposes to work more closely with YO's designers to ensure YO supplies the type of clothing that MX feels its customers want

---

Today is 8th May 20X5

You receive the following email from Rad Cooper, Operations Director of YO.

From: Rad Cooper RC@YO.co.uk
To: Colin Radner CR@YO.co.uk
Sent: 8th May 20X5, 8.00am
Subject: Quality and supply chains

Colin,

As you are aware, MX is a major customer of ours and in the near future we will be entering talks about renegotiating our contract with them.

If these talks are unsuccessful, YO is likely to lose MX's business. We are aware that MX has experimented by using a few trusted overseas suppliers who have managed to achieve both relatively low prices and superior quality through the adoption of Total Quality Management (TQM) techniques.

I am anxious to maintain our company's relationship with MX and I recognise that we must change from our present focus on price to one that includes relationship building and quality considerations.

In preparation for this meeting I would be grateful for your views on two areas.

Firstly, could you evaluate the way in which MX currently manages its suppliers (including YO) as part of a supply chain and how it is proposing to do so in the future.

Secondly, could you explain the main changes which will be required at YO in order to achieve total quality.

Kind regards

Rad

Rad Cooper
Operations Director, YO
E: RC@YO.co.uk
T: 0208 500 6000

Write your response to the email from Rad Cooper

Task 33 - Cranmoor

(indicative timing : 45 mins)

You are Emily Woo and you work for CABRAS, a non-governmental organisation (NGO) in the country of Cranmoor that has an interest in business regulation and the corporate social responsibility of companies.

There is currently a global recession and Cranmoor is facing mounting difficulties including a substantial balance of trade deficit and a weakening economy. The new Government has promised to be 'financially prudent, ethical, and prepared to listen to and be protective of all stakeholder groups in society'.

Government ministers recently met with some leaders of business and commerce where a number of issues were discussed and later published in a national newspaper.

Business leaders expressed the view that there needs to be less Government regulation of markets and a greater focus instead on dealing with the economy.

The Government in return responded by saying that business needs to act more responsibly and that 'good corporate social responsibility (CSR) is good for society, good for business, and good for the human resource policies of individual businesses.

The Government claimed that without good CSR a number of stakeholder groups within society may feel isolated and vulnerable.

The following is an extract from an email sent by Heidi Fly, a senior manager in CABRAS, to other senior managers.

I find it shocking that business leaders in our country feel that the Government should regulate less and just concentrate on economic matters. Surely the point of Government is to control how businesses operate?

As to corporate social responsibility, I cannot believe the Government is suggesting that it is a good thing for business. It is not for businesses to look after a nation's citizens, that is a role of government.

Today is 9th May 20X5

You receive the following email from Luke Walker, a senior manager of CABRAS.

From: Luke Walker LW@CABRAS.co.cr
To: Emily Woo EW@CABRAS.co.cr
Sent: 9th May 20X5, 10.00am
Subject: Government regulation and CSR

Emily,

Members of the senior management team are concerned with recent newspaper reports regarding Government regulation and Corporate Social Responsibility (CSR).

We are having a management meeting in a few days to discuss the issues, and in preparation for this I would be grateful if you could supply me with a briefing that addresses a number of areas.

In particular, I am interested in whether business leaders are correct in saying that Cranmoor's Government should focus less on regulation and instead focus more on dealing with the economy. In regards to CSR, could you explain the benefits an organisation might derive from adhering to good CSR principles in its business activities, and whether there is a relationship between CSR and an organisation's human resource policies.

Luke

Luke Walker
Senior Manager, CABRAS
E: LW@CABRAS.co.uk
T: 0208 700 1000

Write your response to the email from Luke Walker

Task 34 - V

(indicative timing : 45 mins)

This question is based on a real-life company, Virgin. Virgin originally started as a record shop but quickly expanded, and now runs many different types of business including, airlines, holiday companies, gyms, trains, TV, Internet, mobile phones and wines.

It was founded and is still run one of the UK's most successful entrepreneurs and one who is able to keep his companies in the public spotlight through strong public relations campaigns.

Business awareness is important to your CIMA studies and key to answering this question. Therefore you should try to keep yourself up-to-date with the world of business and global brands.

Background information

V is an innovative company, run according to the principles of its entrepreneurial owner. V operates a package distribution service, a train service, and sells holidays, bridal outfits, clothing, mobile telephones, and soft drinks.

V is well known for challenging the norm and 'giving customers quality products and services at affordable prices and doing it all with a sense of fun'. V spends little on advertising, but has great brand awareness thanks to the 'visibility' of its inspirational owner.

V's prices are affordable; but they are not the cheapest in the market because the company is able to charge a premium for its brand. However they are competitive when compared against some other competitors.

V has just announced the launch of 'V-cosmetics' to exploit a gap in the market. The cosmetic range will be competitively priced against high street brands and have the distinctive V logo.

You work for a market analyst and recently attended a press conference where more information concerning V-cosmetics was released. You made the following notes:

V-cosmetics will not be on sale in high street shops. Instead V will use two approaches to promotion and selling, namely:

- The use of 'cosmetic associates'. Individuals may apply to become an associate and, if accepted, will be required to buy a basic stock of every V-cosmetic product. The associate will then use these products as samples and 'testers'. After initial training, associates organise parties in the homes of friends, and their friends, where they take orders for products at a listed price. Associates receive commission based on sales.

- The Internet and mobile telephone technology will also be heavily used to sell V cosmetic products to the public.

You are Lindsay Sullivan and today is 10th May 20X5

You have receive the following email from Brandon Richardson, the market analyst that you work for.

From: Brandon Richardson BR@MKT.co.uk
To: Lindsay Sullington LS@MKT.co.uk
Sent: 10th May 20X5, 11.00am
Subject: V-cosmetics

Lindsay

NTV, our National TV station has asked me if I would like to be interviewed on its 'Business Breakfast' programme to give insights about the thinking behind the V brand's new cosmetics business.

Since you recently attended a press conference and have done some research on the venture I would be grateful if you could email me some notes that cover the following areas:

Firstly, how can V's proposed approach be understood within the context of direct marketing and the marketing mix.

Could you set out the main advantages, to companies such as V, of using the internet as a marketing and sales channel, and how V may use the internet in its marketing approach.

Finally, could you make me aware of the main ethical issues associated with the proposal to market V cosmetics.

Brandon
Brandon Richardson
Senior market analyst, MKT
E: BR@MKT.co.uk
T: 0208 200 9000

Write your response to the email from Brandon

Task 35 - OK4u

(indicative timing : 45 mins)

You are Rachel Smith, the management accountant at OK4u, a national leisure and sports chain selling specialist equipment and clothing for 'every sport'.

A relatively young organisation, all OK4u's growth has been internally generated and has been led by its entrepreneurial founder and Chief Executive Officer (CEO) who is known for his creativity and person centred approach.

Store managers are given discretion to display items in imaginative ways and use promotions to generate sales locally. All store managers report directly to the CEO who tries to oversee all aspects of the organisation's functioning without the help of a management team.

In its advertising, OK4u makes a feature of the creative way in which it is reducing non-recyclable packaging.

It also claims to follow ethical policies. It has a few trusted long term suppliers of sports equipment and clothing. All suppliers are personally known to OK4u's CEO, and some are close friends.

Good logistics mean that valuable floor area is not taken up by excessive in-shop storage. Known for good design, broad appeal and no 'stock outs', OK4u has established itself over the past five years as one of the country's favourite high street brands. Unfortunately, all that changed recently.

A year ago, OK4u expanded its product range by introducing fashion clothing into its stores. This was manufactured by a number of new suppliers. Initially sales were disappointing, until OK4u decided to discount prices. Thanks to tightly negotiated contracts, OK4u was able to pass the costs of the campaign on to its many new suppliers. As sales improved, these same suppliers were pressurised by threats of financial penalties into meeting late orders to tight deadlines.

A national newspaper recently ran a story summarised below:

'The Shame of Sweatshop OK4u'

OK4u uses workers from third world countries and pays them a fraction of the selling price of the goods they produce. In some cases, children as young as eight years old are working long hours.

Following the adverse publicity, sales in all business areas recovered slightly, but they are nowhere near their previous levels. The brand was also voted one of the most poorly regarded in a recent independent survey. The events have also affected morale, and staff turnover has increased.

The CEO investigated the newspaper's claims and sent a memo to all members of staff. Some relevant extracts of the memo are below:

Memo
From: Jeremy Jackson
To: Staff

Following my investigation of the recent newspaper claims, I have the following findings:

- The incidents related to a few of the new fashion range items.

- None of the workers featured in the story were OK4u employees. The fault lay with our new clothing suppliers, some of whom OK4u knew little about.

- In some cases, these new clothing suppliers had sub-contracted work in order to keep costs low and meet delivery deadlines. In doing this, they had exploited vulnerable workers.

As a consequence of this investigation, I am immediately withdrawing the new fashion range and will issue a public apology. I shall explain that the fault was with our suppliers and that we will be more careful in developing new supplier relationships in future.

Today is 11th May 20X5

The CEO sends you the following email.

From: Jeremy Jackson JJ@OK4u.co.uk
To: Rachel Smith RS@OK4u.co.uk
Sent: 11th May 20X5, 9.15am
Subject: Company turnaround

Rachel

I've reviewed our current situation and recognise the need to combat the negative perception that the public has of OK4u. I'm planning on sending a personal letter to all our employees setting out a turnaround plan for our company.

I believe the key to becoming one of the country's favourite high street brands again is to deliver excellent customer satisfaction and that this can be achieved through a superb combination of marketing, HRM and operations. I also believe that a strong performance appraisal system could be an important tool in motivating employees.

In order to plan the turnaround of the company I would be grateful if you could provide me with the following information:

A summary of the main ethical and management failings associated with our expansion into selling fashion clothing.

What measures we might take in order to restore public confidence that we are following ethical and socially responsible policies.

How marketing, HRM and operations in OK4u could deliver 'excellent customer satisfaction'.

In addition, please could you explain the purpose and objectives of performance appraisal, so that I can include these points in my letter to the employees.

Jeremy

Jeremy Jackson
CEO, OK4u
E: JJ@OK4u.co.uk
T: 0208 700 1000

Write your response to the email from Jeremy Jackson

Task 36 - Hubbles

(indicative timing : 45 mins)

You are Geoff Shrewd, a management accountant employed by Hubbles. Hubbles is a national high-street clothing retailer has recently appointed a new Chief Executive. The company is well established and relatively financially secure. It has a reputation for stability and for selling traditional, quality clothing at an affordable price. The company has also recently started to sell goods through a website. Lately, however, it has suffered from intense competition leading to a loss of market share and an erosion of customer loyalty.

Hubbles has all the major business functions provided by 'in house' departments, including finance, human resources, purchasing, strategy and marketing. The Strategy and Marketing Department has identified a need for a comprehensive review of the company's effectiveness.

In response, the new Chief Executive has commissioned a review by management consultants.

Extracts from their initial findings include the following:

- Hubbles has never moved from being sales-oriented to being marketing-oriented and this is why it has lost touch with its customers;

- Hubbles now needs to get closer to its customers and operate a more effective marketing mix;

- Additional investment in its purchasing department can add significantly to improving Hubbles' competitive position.

Today is 12th May 20X5

The Chief Executive of Hubbles sends you the following email.

From: Imogen Nash IN@Hubbles.co.uk

To: Geoff Shrewd GS@Consult.co.uk

Sent: 12th May 20X5, 11.30am

Subject: Presentation

Geoff

Given the review of Hubbles by your team, I feel that a presentation of your interim findings to senior managers would be helpful at this point.

My Personal Assitant will prepare the slides for the presentation, but I need you to provide the technical content. Please could you summarise your key points as a list and include a short note explaining them.

I firstly need an explanation of the difference between a company that concentrates on 'selling' its products and one that has a marketing orientation.

Could you continue by setting out how Hubbles might develop itself into an organisation that is driven by customer needs, and explain the ways in which the management of Hubbles could make use of the marketing mix to help regain its competitive position.

Finally, could you explain the main areas in which Hubbles' Human Resources Department might support its Purchasing Department and how an efficient Purchasing Department might contribute to effective organisational performance.

Kind regards,

Imogen Nash

CEO, Hubbles

E: IN@Hubbles.co.uk

T: 0208 500 2000

Write your response to the email from Imogen Nash

Topic 6 – E1 Further Tasks Solutions

Task 31

Marking scheme

	Marks
Aligning systems and business strategy Up to 2 marks for each relevant, explained point	5
Approaches to implementation Up to 2 marks for each relevant, explained point	5
User involvement Up to 2 marks per valid point referenced to the scenario	5
User training Up to 2 marks per valid point referenced to the scenario	5
5 System evaluation Up to 2 marks per valid point referenced to the scenario	5
	25

Our answer shows what we consider the most appropriate points to make. Other relevant points that answer the question would earn marks. However, irrelevant points that do not answer the question would not earn marks.

Suggested solution

The following points might be helpful when writing your answer.

When considering the fit of a new system with strategy, there are only really two options – change the system or the process.

When looking at approaches to implementation, try to think about the risks and challenges of introducing the system.

User involvement and training is relatively straightforward. Just consider who the users are and their needs regarding the system.

Reviewing the success or failure of the system is very similar to any investment or project. Cost-benefit and performance reviews are obvious suggestions.

From: Miranda Mills MM@SandC.co.uk
To: Paul Perker PP@SandC.co.uk
Sent: 7th May 20X5, 13.50pm
Subject: System implementation

Dear Paul,

In response to your email this morning, I have answered each of your queries in turn below:

Alignment with business strategy

The system is likely to be a source of competitive advantage for the firm because the cost savings and subsequent productivity gains will not be available to its competitors. To make the most of the advantage, it must be aligned with the firm's overall business strategy.

Fitting the software and business processes

S & C has two choices if the software does not fit its business processes.

(1)   Customise the software to the match the processes.

(2)   Change the processes to match the software.

Customise the software

The benefit of this option is that there will be less disruption within the firm as the business processes remain unchanged. However, there could be a large financial cost if external experts have to be brought in or if the changes are complex. There is also a risk that new programming introduces glitches into the system.

Change the processes

This option saves the cost of additional programming and the risk of introducing glitches. However, changing business processes could have a negative impact on the morale and efficiency of the staff as it would represent a major change in the way they work.

Direct and phased approaches to implementation

Direct approach

Under a direct approach, on one particular day the old system is switched off and the new one switched on. There is no overlap or period of dual running of both systems.

Phased approach

A phased approach involves selecting one section of the system at a time for direct changeover. Then when the first section is running satisfactorily, another section of the system is changed over.

Suitability

The phased approach is more suitable than a direct approach because it controls the risk involved when switching over to a new system – this is particularly important as S & C will be introducing a brand new system that no one else has used.

The firm would implement the new system in discrete stages – corresponding to the current system they replace.

This would have the following advantages:

*   Risk is reduced as glitches will be limited to the new subsystem only.

*   Staff will adapt to change more easily as it occurs over a longer period in small chunks.

*   It allows time for feedback from staff involved in earlier phases to be considered when rolling out later ones. For example, small glitches or user-friendliness.

*   There is less disruption so the benefits of the changes can be felt more quickly.

User involvement

User involvement in system implementation is essential to obtain user acceptance. Specific examples of activities users should be involved in include:

Testing

Developers should ask a group of users to test the system to check that it works as it should and actually meet their needs.

Training

The implementation phase is usually towards the end of the development. Users should start their training on the new system so they are prepared for the changeover.

File conversion and transfer

Data within the old system will need to be transferred to the new system. Users should be involved in the transfer as their knowledge will help ensure data is interpreted correctly.

Quality circles and discussions

Forums that include users should be set up to discuss the overall quality of the system and how it could be improved.

Championing change

Users who can see the benefits of the new system should become involved in winning over other users who may resist the change.

Training

There are three distinct groups within S & C who have different training needs.

Senior managers

Senior managers will not be using the system on a day-to-day basis, however, they should have a good basic understanding of it so they understand how the work they review was assembled. Such training could be provided by an executive presentation. Some additional, hands-on training may be required covering how reports are obtained.

Managers

Managers should receive training to enable them to understand the software involved in areas they are responsible for, such as setting up new users and removing users if they leave the company. In particular, they should also focus on security features that prevent unauthorised access or loss or damage to data.

Users

Users need to be trained in the day-to-day features and processes that the system provides. This would include data-entry and report writing amongst others.

Methods of training

These may include:

- In-house demonstrations
- On-line learning
- Computer based training using dummy data

System evaluation

A number of methods can be used to evaluate the success or failure of the system.

Cost-benefit review

Following the completion of the project a cost-benefit review can begin. This analyses the actual costs incurred in developing and implementing the system with the actual benefits the system provides. Benefits can be difficult to quantify so the firm may have to make use of estimates. This review will help determine whether the system is a financial success or failure.

Performance reviews

Performance reviews consider whether the system is performing as expected and may cover issues such as:

- System efficiency – is the system operating quickly enough, does it slow down when processing large volumes of data?

- Security – is the system secure, have there been many breaches?

- Error rates – does data in the system contain errors? If there are then there may be problems in data collection and file conversion.

- Output – does the system produce its output on a timely basis, is it being used as expected, does it go to the right people?

Post-implementation review

This establishes whether or not the system's objectives and targeted performance criteria have been met. It compares the system's actual and predicted performance. Unlike a performance review, a post-implementation review is more of a summary review that is undertaken later on, once any teething problems have been overcome. The contents of this and the other reviews are used in a formal post-implementation review report to judge the system's success or failure.

I hope my explanations above provide the information you require. Please let me know if you require any further information.

Kind Regards,

Miranda

Miranda Mills
Management Accountant, S&C
E: MM@SandC.co.uk
T: 0208 300 4010

Competency coverage

Sub-task	Technical	Business acumen		People		Leadership	Max
1		Aligning systems and business strategy	4	Communication	1		5
2		Approaches to implementation	4	Communication	1		5
3		User involvement	4	Communication	1		5
4		User training	4	Communication	1		5
5		System evaluation	4	Communication	1		5
Total			20		5		25

This question focuses on the key areas related to the implementation of a new computer system and offers students plenty of scope to demonstrate their knowledge. In all sub-tasks, students are required to explain a little theory and then apply it to the scenario. Most of the marks will be awarded for relating knowledge to the scenario. CIMA's competency framework indicates that, for E1, such marks will be awarded for business acumen. There are some minor marks available for communication in each sub-task for choosing an appropriate format for the reply and for language used.

Task 32

Marking scheme

Our answer shows what we consider the most appropriate points to make. Other relevant points that answer the question would earn marks. However, irrelevant points that do not answer the question would not earn marks.

Suggested solution

A way into the first aspect of this question is to set the evaluation in the context of the relevant theory – in this case Porter's value chain. The requirement states that you should look at the current situation and the new strategy so make sure that you do this.

You should ensure that you explain some background principles of TQM in the second part, but don't forget to again consider the current and new strategy before stating a few factors for TQM success.

From: Colin Radner CR@YO.co.uk
To: Rad Cooper RC@YO.co.uk
Sent: 8th May 20X5, 11.00am
Subject: Quality and supply chains

Dear Rad,

I appreciate the importance of these renegotiation talks and have looked into the two areas that you requested. I hope the following information will prove useful to you.

Value system

A value system links the value chains of individual companies together. In Porter's terms, each company has a value chain including inbound logistics, production and outbound logistics. The outbound logistics of one company becomes the inbound logistics of another company.

In our situation, YO provides clothes to MX so the outbound logistic system of YO is therefore linked to the inbound logistic systems of MX. Similarly, we at YO receive inputs from our own suppliers linking inbound logistics back to those suppliers.

Value chain management

Management of the value chain between companies is essential to create and maintain competitive advantage. If YO fails to supply the correct goods, or supplies the correct goods late, then MX's sales will be affected. It is in the best interests of all companies in the supply value chain to ensure products pass along the chain in a timely fashion and appropriate quality is maintained.

Current strategy

MX's current strategy regarding suppliers has been multiple sourcing – this means that the same inputs are obtained from a number of different suppliers. This decreases individual supplier power, as MX can choose which supplier to purchase from. However, YO is heavily dependent on MX – 80% of YO's sales being made to MX. This means MX has additional power over YO – YO cannot afford to lose MX as a customer. MX's policy of paying low prices and returning goods not up to specification is therefore not surprising.

New strategy

MX is now considering limiting the number of suppliers, improving the quality of inputs and paying more per garment purchased. This change indicates that MX wants to be more actively involved in the supply chain and improve product quality for the benefit of both MX and YO. MX is sacrificing some supplier power (few suppliers to purchase from) for a better supplier relationship. This strategy should help to provide more competitive advantage for YO/MX's products.

Total Quality Management

Quality - YO's current position

Currently, YO focuses on producing clothes at a relatively low price, because our major customer, MX, has the strategy of selling large volumes at low prices. However, MX is now moving more 'upmarket' which means that the company is attempting to sell goods of a higher quality at a slightly higher price. This has the effect that MX expects a higher quality of inputs and is now rejecting inputs which are below this new quality standard.

Quality - new requirements

From YO's point-of-view, production at high quality but low price is difficult. Provision of a higher quality output implies that the customer is prepared to pay for this quality, and it does not appear that MX is prepared to raise prices significantly at present. YO therefore needs to raise quality for the same price. One method that some of MX's suppliers have used to do this is Total Quality Management (TQM), which is a technique that YO can consider using.

TQM involves the development of an organisational culture in which all members of staff have an interest in, and are responsible for, the quality of the work that they produce.

Quality system

YO will need to implement a three stage system to monitor the quality of clothes produced.

(1)   Inspection of the final product to detect quality errors

(2)   Set quality standards and assess performance against those standards

(3)   Extend quality management to all areas of the company, not just focus on production. For example, ensuring that design quality is maintained/improved.

Factors for the successful use of TQM include:

Quality culture

A culture of quality is required involving all staff from senior management to production workers. Because of the importance of MX as YO's major customer, all management levels need to be committed to success of TQM.

Empowerment/training

All employees should be encouraged to avoid mistakes (rather than detecting them), and should be empowered to improve quality where they can. This also means that YO must provide training for employees in how to implement and use TQM techniques.

Continuous improvement

Improving quality must be seen as an ongoing process, not a one-off change. Policies such as quality circles and communication of quality objectives are required to ensure the ongoing success of TQM.

Kind regards,

Colin
Colin Radner
Management Accountant, YO
E: CR@YO.co.uk
T: 0208 550 6600

Competency coverage

Sub-task	Technical	Business acumen		People		Leadership	Max
1		Supply chain management	8	Communication	2		10
2		Total quality management	13	Communication	2		15
Total			21		4		25

This question requires students to draw on their business acumen by analysing the company's current situation and projecting what the new developments will bring. In all sub-tasks, students are required to explain a little theory and then apply it to the scenario. Most of the marks will be awarded for relating knowledge to the scenario. CIMA's competency framework indicates that, for E1, such marks will be awarded for business acumen. There are some minor marks available for communication in each sub-task for choosing an appropriate format for the reply and for language used.

Task 33

Marking scheme

	Marks
Need for government regulation Up to 1 mark for each relevant, explained point	10
Benefits of CSR Up to 2 marks for each relevant, explained point	8
CSR and HR Up to 1 mark per valid point , explained point	7
	25

Our answer shows what we consider the most appropriate points to make. Other relevant points that answer the question would earn marks. However, irrelevant points that do not answer the question would not earn marks.

Suggested solution

The secret to answering this question is to set out a structure for your answer before you begin to write. In the first part, a good place to start is by splitting your answer between 'regulation' and 'economic matters'.

The final two parts focus on CSR, firstly general benefits and secondly the relationship between CSR and HR policies. Be careful not to repeat information here. If you get stuck, think about the various business areas (such as operations and marketing) and come up with some reasonable benefits that CSR might bring. In the final part think about the various aspects of HR (recruitment, development and motivation) and consider how CSR might affect them.

From: Emily Woo EW@CABRAS.co.cr
To: Luke Walker LW@CABRAS.co.cr
Sent: 9th May 20X5, 14.00pm
Subject: Government regulation and CSR

Luke

I've looked into your request and the views I have on the issues are described below:

Regulation and economic matters

The business leaders of Cranmoor have suggested that the Government should regulate markets less and concentrate on economic matters. I shall consider each point in turn.

Market regulation

Market regulation can be defined as any form of state interference with the operation of the free market.

Governments regulate industries in order to balance the needs of the customer (which are not always being met) with the needs of the industry (which is usually profit maximisation). The goal of regulation is to ensure safe products and services are available without inhibiting the function and development of the industry that provides them.

Regulation in Cranmoor

Those who advocate the reduction of legislation (such as the business leaders of Cranmoor) believe that the free market will allocate resources effectively, and encourage businesses to become efficient due to increased competition.

Businesses that are subject to less regulation will not encounter costs of meeting regulatory requirements and should therefore be more profitable.

However, those in favour of regulation cite the need to enforce competition, where the market is not competitive, and to improve the quality and quantity of goods and services provided, where the industry does not meet the needs of the customer.

Economic matters

Governments have a macroeconomic policy that usually is based around four objectives. These objectives are a controlled balance of trade, economic growth, controlled inflation and low unemployment. Cranmoor currently has a substantial balance of payments deficit and a weakening economy, so these areas are of prime concern.

Balance of trade

The balance of trade reflects a country's trading position and concerns the amount that it exports as against how much it imports. Cranmoor's balance of trade deficit indicates that the country is importing more than it is exporting.

It is therefore very important that the Government seeks to reduce this deficit by increasing exports in relation to imports.

Economic growth

A country's economic growth refers to the level of demand for goods and services within the economy and how much is being produced. Cranmoor's weakening economy indicates that demand for goods is falling and the amount of goods being produced is also falling.

The Government should therefore seek to improve growth, perhaps by looking to increase the disposable income of its citizens (by reducing taxation) or stimulating demand by investing in infrastructure projects.

Inflation

Inflation refers to the rate at which the price of goods and services changes over time. Rising inflation means the price of goods and services is increasing and this can be a consequence of too much demand within the economy. Those on fixed incomes, such as those on pensions or state benefits, are the hardest hit in times of inflation.

Cranmoor's Government should seek to prevent inflation becoming a problem when the economy improves by managing demand so that prices do not rise too quickly.

Employment

High employment is a key goal of any Government. This is because it means the amount it receives from personal taxation is maximised and the amount that it pays out in state benefits is minimised. It also means that citizens have more disposable income and therefore can spend more, fuelling economic growth. Cranmoor's Government should establish policies that encourage job creation in order to support its other macroeconomic goals.

Conclusion

Cranmoor's Government should certainly concentrate on the economic matters described above. Whether it should regulate less depends on specific industries. Some may be competitive and meet the needs of the consumer, others may not. Regulation should be limited to industries that need it.

Benefits of Corporate Social Responsibility policies

Corporate social responsibility (CSR) refers to the expectation in society that companies are accountable for the social and ethical effects of their actions.

The government of Cranmoor has stated that without good CSR a number of stakeholder groups within its society may feel isolated and vulnerable. This suggests that Cranmoor's businesses are not currently always acting in the interests of wider society when making business decisions and it may be because they do not appreciate the possible benefits to them of behaving in a socially responsible manner.

Benefits to an organisation of adhering to good CSR principles

The following are benefits good CSR may bring to a business.

Improved corporate image

The adoption of good CSR policies will demonstrate to customers and potential customers that the business is forward looking and is proactive in dealing with changes in society and the environment. This is especially true where a business changes its behaviours before it is required to (ie before legislation on that particular area comes into force). This will create a positive view of the business within the market.

Marketing

An improved corporate image will enable the business to differentiate its products and services from those of the competition because the brand and its values become a unique selling point. Public relations (PR) is a key part of the promotion mix and therefore improved public relations that result from the CSR policies will present the business with an increased range of marketing possibilities.

Branding

A business may build a brand based on strong ethical and socially responsible values. Such values may contribute to brand equity and the value of the brand, as well as the long-term success of the company. This is because the business may be able to gain and retain customers because they share the brand's values and will stick with the organisation in good times and bad.

Efficient operations

Many socially responsible policies, such as improving recycling and reducing waste, will have a secondary benefit of improving the efficiency of business operations.

Pricing

A strong brand and CSR values may enable the business to charge a premium for its goods and services above that of its competitors. This is because customers may accept a higher price in return for buying into the organisation's values. Therefore the organisation will have some flexibility in its pricing decisions with the possibility of increasing its revenues whilst maintaining its customer base.

Profitability

Potentially increased revenues and reduced costs as identified above will together improve the organisation's profitability.

Corporate Social Responsibility and Human Resource policies

Human resource policies concern how an organisation recruits, develops, rewards, motivates and develops its culture. They are linked to CSR policies since they both concern people.

Recruitment

A strong, socially responsible brand will help the business not only attract and retain customers, but also staff as well. Employees may be attracted by the organisation, particularly if they share its values and may decide to work for it rather than other, less socially responsible organisations. The quality of staff may also rise as a consequence.

Development

Socially responsible businesses see their employees as people rather than just a number. They take an interest in improving their employees, not only in terms of what is needed in their current career, but also other areas of personal development.

Reward

In recent times there has been a move to socially responsible rewards and benefits offered to employees. For example, home working, flexible working, the living wage and support for gym memberships and childcare.

Culture

Socially responsible businesses often have a culture with a positive outlook, a 'can-do' attitude and support for philanthropic activities (for example allowing employees time off to undertake voluntary work). Such a culture will feed into the corporation's external image (supporting the business and recruitment of employees) and the motivation of existing staff.

Motivation

The combination of corporate culture, development and reward discussed above should help motivate employees. This extra motivation should help improve business productivity, reduce absenteeism and aid staff retention. These will have cost benefits to the business in the long-run.

I hope this information proves useful.

Kind regards,

Emily

Emily Woo
Management Accountant, CABRAS
E: LW@CABRAS.co.uk
T: 0208 770 1100

Competency coverage

Sub-task	Technical	Business acumen		People		Leadership	Max
1		Need for government regulation	8	Communication	2		10
2		Benefits of CSR	6	Communication	2		8
3		CSR and HR	6	Communication	1		7
Total			20		5		25

This question requires students to consider the interaction of the government with business and of the effect of corporate social responsibility. In the first sub-task, students are required to explain a little theory and then apply it to the scenario. In the other two sub-tasks, most of the marks are awarded for relevant points, but there is less need for application. CIMA's competency framework indicates that, for E1, such marks will be awarded for business acumen. There are some minor marks available for communication in each sub-task for choosing an appropriate format for the reply and for language used.

Task 34

Marking scheme

	Marks
Explaining V's approach to marketing Up to 1 mark for each relevant point	8
Advantages of using the Internet as a sales channel Up to 1 mark for each relevant point	5
Explaining how V can use the Internet Up to 1 mark for each relevant point	6
Explaining the ethical issues regarding V cosmetics Up to 1 mark for each relevant point	6
	25

Our answer shows what we consider the most appropriate points to make. Other relevant points that answer the question would earn marks. However, irrelevant points that do not answer the question would not earn marks.

This question focuses on a number of topical issues, e-commerce and ethical considerations of marketing. In sub-task 1, students are required to explain a little marketing theory and then apply it to the scenario. Most of the marks will be awarded for relating the marketing mix to the scenario. Sub-task 2 just requires the listing of textbook knowledge in regards to advantages of e-commerce. Sub-tasks 3 and 4 both require the application of knowledge to the scenario. CIMA's competency framework indicates that, for E1, such marks will be awarded for business acumen. There are some minor marks available for communication in each sub-task for choosing an appropriate format for the reply and for language used.

Suggested solution

Although this question focuses on marketing you are also required to discuss ethical implications as well. You should always be prepared for questions such as this that cover a range of syllabus areas.

In the first part, a good structure would be to define marketing and the marketing mix before using the marketing mix to analyse the product.

You could attempt the second part by using basic textbook knowledge of the Internet but you should relate your points to the scenario.

The last part on ethics should really be based on the scenario. It should not be too difficult to spot a few areas that have ethical implications.

From: Lindsay Sullington LS@MKT.co.uk
To: Brandon Richardson BR@MKT.co.uk
Sent: 10th May 20X5, 17.00pm
Subject: V-cosmetics

Brandon

In response to your email I have written the following notes.

Direct marketing and the marketing mix

Direct marketing

Direct marketing is a concept that involves the producer of a product interacting directly with the end customer or consumer. The approach can be summed up as 'cutting out the middle-man'.

It is sometimes referred to as a 'zero level channel', as there are zero levels between supplier and the end customer.

Internet

The internet has enabled more businesses to utilise direct marketing. For example, an airline such as Virgin Atlantic Airways may sell tickets direct to the public via its own website (selling flights via a general travel website isn't 'pure' direct marketing as this involves an intermediary – even if that intermediary happens to be based on the web).

Marketing mix

The traditional marketing mix includes Product, Price, Promotion and Place. Each of these factors play an important part in the overall offering to customers. V's proposed approach can be understood in this context.

Product

V's products are good quality, fun products with a strong brand. It is important the cosmetics offered are consistent with the established reputation of the brand.

Price

Pricing is competitive, but not the cheapest (ie affordable to most). An important decision is whether the 'list price' will include a mark-up to enable agents to offer discounting. Website sales may be offered at a lower price – although this may make party purchases less attractive to customers.

Promotion

V will rely on word of mouth, public relations (such as the TV interview) and the strength of the brand.

Place

V's distribution strategy is to use one level marketing (the cosmetic associates) and some web sales. This relies upon the skill of associates and user acceptance of e-commerce. V also needs efficient transportation options (eg partner a courier business) to ensure order fulfilment.

Advantages of the internet as a marketing channel include the following:

- Communication is quick, allowing rapid response to customer orders/queries
- The range of tasks able to be performed eg promotion, display products, e-commerce
- Enables quick price and feature comparison for customers
- Can lower costs through reduced need for physical outlets
- Provides an opportunity for global reach even for very small organisations
- Facilitates information collection and developing customer databases for future promotions
- Customer convenience, as it may be accessed from home or work at any time

Use of the internet in V's marketing mix

V could use the internet in the following ways.

E-commerce

A website with an e-commerce capability would enable orders to be submitted and paid for on-line (using credit and debit cards). This means that customers can order V's products from wherever they are rather than being limited to buying them from a high street store. Efficient order fulfilment is vital.

Product information

The website could also be used to provide detailed product information to customers, for example the ingredients of different cosmetic products (particularly relevant to those with allergies) provide cosmetic advice and related discussion groups.

Corporate information

General information about V as a group and about V cosmetics could also be communicated in this way – helping to cultivate the idea of a 'fun' organisation.

Promotion

The site could be used for promotion using web banners and could include links to 'partners' sites and a search facility (eg access to Google from within V's site).

Target marketing

Micro-site capability for specific target audiences (such as teenagers or mature customers) or cosmetic needs (such as hiding birth marks or wrinkles) could be established.

Ethical considerations for V-cosmetics

Ethics is concerned with right and wrong – acting responsibly and with a sense of fairness. The main ethical issues associated with Vs proposal are:

Will the cosmetics be tested on animals – and if so will associates and customers be informed?

Where and how will the products be produced? Will this involve factories in developing countries – what about employment conditions, worker remuneration, waste disposal? Will the company tell customers about where and how the products are produced?

Are associates treated fairly? What mark-up is V making? Will they be supported after their initial training?

Is it acceptable to target customers through mobile phones? This could be seen as intrusive and an abuse of personal information.

Is party selling ethical? V should consider the blurring of business and pleasure and the use of alcohol at the parties. Are people pressured into attending and then made to feel they should 'join in' and buy?

I hope this information is useful to you.

Kind regards,

Lindsay

Lindsay Sullington
Management Accountant, MKT
E: LS@MKT.co.uk T: 0208 240 9900

Competency coverage

Sub-task	Technical	Business acumen		People		Leadership	Max
1		Explaining V's approach to marketing	6	Communication	2		8
2		Advantages of using the Internet as a sales channel	4	Communication	1		5
3		Explaining how V can use the Internet	5	Communication	1		6
4		Explaining the ethical issues regarding V cosmetics	5	Communication	1		6
Total			20		5		25

BPP
LEARNING MEDIA

Task 35

Marking scheme

	Marks
Ethical and managerial failings Up to 1 mark for each relevant, explained point	5
Methods to restore public confidence Up to 1 mark for each relevant, explained point	5
Delivering customer satisfaction Up to 2 marks for each relevant, explained point, referenced to the scenario	10
Purpose and objectives of performance appraisal Up to 1 mark for each relevant, explained point	5
	25

Our answer shows what we consider the most appropriate points to make. Other relevant points that answer the question would earn marks. However, irrelevant points that do not answer the question would not earn marks.

Suggested solution

When attempting this question, look for opportunities to break your answer down into smaller parts. For example, in the first aspect you could break your answer down into ethical and managerial failings. In the third aspect, use marketing, HRM and operations as headings and consider how each contributes to customer satisfaction.

Your answer to the second aspect on ethics and CSR could cover a wide range of areas. Providing they are relevant and link back to the scenario you will earn marks.

The final aspect on appraisal just requires you to relate some textbook knowledge to the company.

From: Rachel Smith RS@OK4u.co.uk
To: Jeremy Jackson JJ@OK4u.co.uk
Sent: 11th May 20X5, 11.15am
Subject: Company turnaround

Jeremy

In response to your email I'm providing the following information.

Ethical failings

Making late orders and threatening financial penalties

OK4u made late orders to its fashion suppliers and used the threat of financial penalties to force them into meeting tight deadlines. Putting suppliers under such pressure is unfair and bad business practice.

Not researching where new suppliers source their products

Companies which follow ethical policies usually look into where new suppliers source their products very carefully and even stipulate that they should avoid using sub-contractors that themselves do not meet certain ethical standards. OK4u did not make such investigations.

Managerial failings

No management team

Due to the rapid growth of OK4u, it must be difficult for one person to devote enough time to all business areas, and with hindsight perhaps a management team could have been brought in to help you run the organisation. A purchasing director would have had the time to look into the new suppliers in more detail and may have been able to identify the ethical issues before they became a problem.

Choosing to increase sales by discounting alone

Reducing prices is not the only way to increase sales. Promotions and advertising could also have a similar effect and OK4u should have looked into using them. The use of such methods would not have put pressure on the suppliers to reduce costs and may have prevented them from using sweat shop labour.

Claiming OK4u follows ethical policies

Despite claiming to follow ethical policies, there is no evidence of such policies being implemented by OK4u's management. It appears that our company's claims are just for marketing purposes and are not backed up by managerial action.

Measures to restore public confidence

Appoint a social responsibility director

We should appoint a director with responsibility for corporate ethical and social responsibility policies. For added public confidence a well known or respected figure could be awarded the role.

Develop an ethical or social responsibility policy

The above director should develop ethical or social responsibility policies which are comprehensive and sincere.

Gain store management support for the policy

Store management should be seen by the public to be supportive and enthusiastic for the policy otherwise they will question its merits.

Train and support employees in following the policy

Ethical or social responsibility policies are ineffective unless they form part of the corporate culture and are implemented by employees in their working lives. Therefore training and support should be given to all to achieve this.

Publicise the steps the company is taking in developing and following the policy

The public must be made aware of the changes that the company has made, for example by taking out adverts in national newspapers. To be successful it is important for the company to be sincere. If the policy appears to be for marketing or 'damage limitation' purposes then the publicity could backfire and damage the company further.

Delivering excellent customer satisfaction

Marketing

OK4u was known for good product design and broad appeal which established it as one of the country's favourite high street brands. Branding sets customer expectations in areas such as image, price, service and values. Customer satisfaction is achieved by meeting or exceeding such expectations.

OK4u should reassess its brand image to ensure it is sending out the right expectations to customers so they are not disappointed when they visit its shops.

Generally customers will be satisfied if they feel that they have received value for money (even if the product or service is priced higher than competitors). This is not just in terms of the product purchased but is also related to the service received and corporate branding.

OK4u should review its price setting strategy to ensure it is in line with customer expectations. It may be that a discounting policy should be avoided in the future because it cheapens the value of the brand.

HRM

It is important that nothing OK4u's customers experience when they visit one of its shops contradict the corporate culture, in particular, the new ethical stance. All employees must be seen to embody the ethical culture. This is because customers may be attracted to OK4u because of its ethical policies and much of their satisfaction will come from knowing they are supporting an ethical company.

Staff training is important, especially in relation to sports equipment. Much customer satisfaction will be achieved by providing expert advice on which products are most suitable for an individual's needs.

OK4u should ensure all staff receive suitable training on all products sold in order to provide excellent levels of advice.

Operations

An aspect of the company's initial success was that it never had any 'stock outs'. Customers are unlikely to be happy if they make a special trip to one of OK4u's stores to find that it has sold out of the one item they need. Good operations management will monitor stock and reorder levels and schedule deliveries before goods run out.

It is important that the organisation focuses on quality of its goods. If products are of poor quality, this will damage the brand, and any associated customer loyalty.

Staff should focus their attention on providing good service to the customer. Measures of customer service could be taken and targets for satisfaction levels set, by which staff performance can be analysed.

Appraisal systems

Purpose of an appraisal system

Performance appraisal is 'the regular and systematic review of performance and the assessment of potential with the aim of producing action programmes to develop both work and individuals.'

The general purpose of any assessment or appraisal system is to improve the efficiency of the organisation by ensuring that the individual employees are performing to the best of their ability and developing their potential for improvement.

Objectives of an appraisal system

The main objectives of an appraisal system are:

- To establish what the individual has to do in a job in order that the objectives for the section or department are realised.

- To assess an individual's current level of job performance.

- To assess the level of reward payable for an individual's efforts, eg, in merit payment systems.

- To assess potential for career and succession planning.

- To identify staff training and development needs and fill skill and performance gaps in the organisation.

I trust that this is sufficient for your needs, please let me know if I can be of any further assistance.

Kind regards,

Rachel

Rachel Smith
Management Accountant, OK4u
E: RS@OK4u.co.uk
T: 0208 740 1700

Competency coverage

Sub-task	Technical	Business acumen		People		Leadership	Max
1		Ethical and managerial failings	4	Communication	1		5
2		Methods to restore public confidence	4	Communication	1		5
3		Delivering customer satisfaction	8	Communication	2		10
4		Purpose and objectives of performance appraisal	4	Communication	1		5
Total			20		5		25

This question really draws on a student's business awareness, but also tests some popular areas of the syllabus that should be familiar to all students. In sub-tasks 1, 2, and 3, students are required to apply their knowledge to the scenario. Most of the marks will be awarded for this. CIMA's competency framework indicates that, for E1, such marks will be awarded for business acumen. There are some minor marks available for communication in each sub-task for choosing an appropriate format for the reply and for language used.

Task 36

Marking scheme

	Marks
Differences between selling and marketing orientations Up to 1 mark for each relevant point	5
Hubbles' development into a company driven by customer needs Up to 1 mark for each relevant point	5
How Hubbles can use the marketing mix to regain competitive position Up to 1 mark for each relevant point	5
How HR can support the purchasing department Up to 1 mark for each relevant point	5
How an efficient purchasing department contributes to effective organisational performance Up to 1 mark for each relevant point	5
	25

Our answer shows what we consider the most appropriate points to make. Other relevant points that answer the question would earn marks. However, irrelevant points that do not answer the question would not earn marks.

Suggested solution:

This question asks for information that will be used in a slide presentation and brief accompanying notes. Therefore you are effectively being asked for a list of headings and a number of sub-headings. Keep your notes brief – this will help your time allocation and keep your answer focussed.

If you get stuck, think about each topic carefully and see if you can come up with suitable headings. For example the marketing mix provides you with some ready-made headings to use and when considering HR, think about the various HR activities.

From: Geoff Shrewd GS@Consult.co.uk
To: Imogen Nash IN@Hubbles.co.uk
Sent: 12th May 20X5, 17.00pm
Subject: Presentation

Imogen

In response to your email I have prepared the following technical notes.

Sales orientation v marketing orientation

Companies with a sales orientation

- 'Let's sell what we've made'

- A focus on advertising, selling and sales promotion but without properly understanding customers' requirements.

Companies with a marketing orientation

- 'Let's make what the customer wants'

- All employees, and the organisation as a whole, have a 'customer focus'

Note. Hubbles' emphasis on 'selling' implies that not enough effort has been made to establish what customers want. If Hubbles markets items that 'strike a cord' with customers, the products should 'sell themselves'.

A marketing orientation for Hubbles

- Find out what customers want – market research

- What (and how) are competitors supplying?

- Compare customer wants with all items currently on the market – any gap could be an opportunity

- Establishing a true marketing orientation will require new ways of working, commitment from staff at all levels and a change of culture

- Some staff may not be suited to the new way of working and may have to leave; others will require information and training

Note. Adopting a marketing orientation will require Hubbles to change how and why decisions are taken. The driving force behind Hubbles' products, markets, prices, and communication must be customer needs. All staff at all levels must see their roles in the context of how Hubbles satisfies or delights customers.

Hubbles and the marketing mix

- Product. Identify what products customers want and ensure they are in stock when customers want to buy them.

- Place. Make it as easy as possible for customers to purchase Hubbles products. Ensure widespread distribution; offer on-line sales with next day delivery.

- Promotion. Get the message out that Hubbles has listened and has changed. Likely to require advertising campaigns using different media to target groups.

- Price. Revise pricing strategy to match the new products. Decide the balance between competing on style and quality or on price.

- People. Reorganise along customer-focussed lines. Encourage customer-focussed culture through training programmes, incentives and staff empowerment.

Note. Hubbles must develop a marketing mix that precisely matches the needs of potential customers in the target market. Research the market for data relating to the age, income, and sex of target market, preferences for product features and attitudes to competitors' products.

Human resources helping purchasing

- Recruiting – ensuring people employed are suited to the role

- Job design – establishing clear responsibilities

- Development and motivation – developing training, appraisal and reward/incentive programmes that result in capable, motivated staff

- Discipline and conflict resolution – providing a framework to limit the possible adverse effects of misconduct and conflict

Note. HR issues are important in all departments, including purchasing. The purchasing department plays a crucial role at Hubbles in the procurement of materials and finished goods for sale, supplier selection and relationships, and price negotiation. HR must ensure the purchasing department has people with the right attitude and skills to perform these tasks.

The purchasing department and organisational performance

- Supplier selection, links and relationships. Establishing supplier selection criteria, quality standards, extranet links, electronic data interchange (EDI)

- Supplier contract negotiation. Guaranteed delivery times and quality enables Just in Time (JIT) production methods to be used

- Co-ordinating purchasing activities to maximise discounts

- Relationship management to encourage mutual co-operation and benefits with suppliers – possible development of a supply network

Note. The purchasing function is now recognised as being crucial to organisational success, particularly in relation to the creation of value and in supply chain management. Purchasing policies that build close relationships with trusted suppliers should result in higher quality – which customers demand. Effective purchasing policies therefore help meet customer needs, which is key to achieving organisational goals.

I trust that this is sufficient for your needs, please let me know if I can be of any further assistance.

Geoff

Geoff Shrewd
Consultant
E: GS@Consult.co.uk
T: 0208 200 5000 Competency coverage

Competency coverage

Sub-task	Technical	Business acumen		People		Leadership	Max
1		Differences between selling and marketing orientations	4	Communication	1		5
2		Hubbles' development into a company driven by customer needs	4	Communication	1		5
3		How Hubbles can use the marketing mix to regain competitive position	4	Communication	1		5
4		How HR can support the purchasing department	4	Communication	1		5
5		How an efficient purchasing department contributes to effective organisational performance	4	Communication	1		5
Total			20		5		25

This question draws on knowledge of HR, marketing and operations management. In all sub-tasks, students are required to apply their knowledge to the scenario. CIMA's competency framework indicates that, for E1, such marks will be awarded for business acumen. There are some minor marks available for communication in each sub-task for choosing an appropriate format for the reply and for language used. It is important that the answer is in an appropriate form to be used as the basis for a presentation.

BPP
LEARNING MEDIA

Topic 7 – Bringing it all together

7 Bringing it all together

Overview

By this point in your ICS studies you have developed your:

- Understanding of the anatomy of an ICS Task
- ICS specific exam technique
  - Time management at Task level
  - Identifying the requirement
  - Planning your answer in context
  - Speaking to your audience
- Ability to move between pillars of the Level in a coherent way

> **You are now ready to bring this together with the real preseen case study to help you fine-tune your approach to your ICS exam**

ICS Real Preseen Exam Kit

We recommend that you insert your ICS Real Preseen Exam Kit into your Workbook at this point.

As you work through it you can then refer back to the Workbook Topics to ensure you integrate the case study information with your learning to date.

The Kit will contain: -

- The real preseen case study
- BPP's analysis of the case study
- Our guidance on how to build the case study into your further preparations for the real exam
- Full mock exam based on the real preseen, with full suggested solutions and marking scheme

BPP
LEARNING MEDIA